LIFE'S JOURNEY

RESOURCES FOR RE, KEY STAGE 2, YEAR 6

JOHN FARADAY

Illustrated by **Anne Sears**

First published in 2000 by
KEVIN MAYHEW LTD
Buxhall, Stowmarket
Suffolk IP14 3BW

© 2000 John Faraday and Anne Sears

The right of John Faraday and Anne Sears to be identified
as the authors of this work has been asserted by them in
accordance with the Copyright, Designs and Patents Act 1988.

The worksheets on pages 24-69 may be photocopied without
copyright infringement, provided they are used for the purpose
for which they were intended. Reproduction of any of the
contents of this book for commercial purposes is subject
to the usual copyright restrictions.

No other part of this publication may be reproduced, stored
in a retrieval system, or transmitted, in any form or by any
means, electronic, mechanical, photocopying, recording or
otherwise, without the prior written permission of the publisher.
All rights reserved.

Scriptures quoted from the Good News Bible, published by
The Bible Societies/HarperCollins Publishers Ltd, UK.
© American Bible Society, 1966, 1971, 1976, 1992.

0 1 2 3 4 5 6 7 8 9

ISBN 1 84003 647 8
Catalogue No 1500393

Cover design by Jonathan Stroulger
Illustrated by Anne Sears
Edited and typeset by Elisabeth Bates

Contents

General note	4
Acknowledgements	4
Foreword	5
How to use this book	7
Using the Bible – where to start	9
Lesson Notes	13
Worksheets	24-69

Lesson 1	Who is God?	
Lesson 2	The birth of Jesus	
Lesson 3	Mary's hopes and fears	
Lesson 4	John the Baptist and the hope of the people	
Lesson 5	Exodus and Passover	
Lesson 6	The Last Supper	
Lesson 7	Who is Jesus?	
Lesson 8	Crowds cheer Jesus!	
Lesson 9	Easter – the victory shown!	
Lesson 10	Ascension	
Lesson 11	Pentecost	
Lesson 12	Baptism and Confirmation	
Lesson 13	Proclamation	
Lesson 14	Loving action	
Lesson 15	Putting faith into practice	
Lesson 16	Faith in action – Saint Paul	
Lesson 17	Faith in action – Francis of Assisi	
Lesson 18	Faith in action – John Wesley	
Lesson 19	Faith in action – Mother Teresa of Calcutta	
Lesson 20	Rules and guidelines – the Ten Commandments	
Lesson 21	Rules and guidelines – Jesus sums up the Law	
Lesson 22	Rules and guidelines – the Beatitudes	
Lesson 23	Rules and guidelines – the fruit of the Spirit	

Answers	70

General note

This book is based on the Blackburn Diocesan Syllabus for Religious Education lessons for Year 6. Its contents will be useful for the Christian side of RE lessons for many syllabuses.

Thanks to . . .

My family (Joan, my wife, and sons Alan, Ian and Andrew) for their love, help, guidance and amazing patience as the book has taken shape.

Anne Sears, whose artwork makes the book special.

The officers of the Blackburn Diocesan Board of Education, in particular Michael Ranyard, Cyril Ashton (now Bishop of Doncaster), Mary Binks, John Hall (now General Secretary of the Church of England Board of Education) and Lisa Fenton for their kind help and guidance.

The people of the Church in Bettws Gwerfil Goch, for their hospitality while I was there to write this book.

Revd Keith and Rita Horsfall, and David and Pauline Cooper for helping with accommodation.

Susan Garnett, Keith Moody, Susan Mawhood, Neil Tattersall, Judith Holden and all the teachers of Saint James' School, Darwen, for their tolerance of my teaching, and their invaluable advice.

Geoff Ainsworth for proof-reading.

The children of Saint James' School, unwitting 'guinea-pigs' as the book was developed.

The people of Saint James' Church, Darwen, for giving me time off to work on the book. I am grateful to them and the diocese for generous gifts during this period.

God, who makes all things possible.

Foreword

There is evidence that the quality of teaching RE at Key Stages 1 and 2 is improving, so the more resources on Christianity that become available the better. This book is a welcome addition to the growing resources available for the teaching of Christianity.

It is always helpful to have a resource that focuses on key areas of Christianity and then offers a range of activities from which teachers can select tasks appropriate to the age and ability of pupils.

Religious Education, when well taught and well resourced, provides pupils with opportunities to develop their own attitudes and thinking on the central issues of life and death. It will also introduce them to the academic rigour necessary if the discipline of religious study is to be of benefit to the pupils. This resource book is another brick in the foundation wall to enable that to happen.

The Revd Canon John R. Hall

General Secretary of the Church of England Board of Education and the National Society (Church of England) for Promoting Religious Education

How to use this book

Preparation time often makes a lesson a successful one, but there are many pressures on teachers' time, and so one of the purposes of this book is to provide helpful RE lessons which need just a minimum of preparation time. It should always be remembered that the main purpose of RE lessons is not to pass school tests (important as these are) but to offer a joyful preparation for life.

The lessons are set out on facing pages which are to be photocopied back to back and given to the pupils as their worksheets. The information comes from various sources and the teacher should be acquainted with this information.

Teacher's preparation

1. The worksheets are designed to interest the child and to contain much of the information needed by both teacher and child. Each child should receive a copy of these sheets, and the teacher should prepare for the lesson by being familiar with the sheets.

2. Puzzle answers are at the back of the book.

3. The Bible* is the main guidebook for Christians, and the lessons relate Bible material to the moral, theological and historical events recorded. The Bible is in two main parts – the Old Testament, which was written over a long period concluding at about 400 or 300 BC; the New Testament, which is about the life and work of Jesus Christ, and the results of his work. It was probably all written in the first century AD, though some parts may have been written in the early second century AD.

4. Other literature may prove helpful, particularly when dealing with non-biblical figures of the past and present.

5. Notes for individual lessons are included to help preparation.

*The Good News Bible, Second edition (Copyright 1994), is the translation used in *Life's Journey*. It will be most useful if copies are available for the pupils, but it may be necessary to write passages on the blackboard or (if copyright permission can be obtained) to photocopy passages. It is essential to use this translation for the puzzles as the wording of other translations may not fit the spaces available on question sheets.

Using the Bible – where to start . . .

In *Life's Journey,* Bible verses are written in the following manner:

Name of book – Number of chapter – Colon(:) – Number of verse

An example of this is **Isaiah 6:3**. First, find the book of Isaiah. The Contents page at the front of the Bible tells us where it starts. All the pages of the book have 'Isaiah' at the top of each page, together with the first and last chapters of facing pages. The sixth chapter of Isaiah has a large number 6 at the beginning. The number after the colon is the verse number. The small numbers in the text are at the start of the appropriate verses. So Isaiah 6:3 reads:

> 'They were calling out to each other:
> "Holy, holy, holy!
> The Lord almighty is holy!
> His glory fills the world."'

Some books have numbers in front of the name. For instance, 2 Kings is the Second book of Kings, not Kings, chapter 2.

There are a number of divisions of books in the Bible. The most obvious being the Old and New Testaments. Some copies of the Bible restart the numbering of pages in the New Testament, so advise the pupils to be careful when looking for a particular page number if that is the case.

Bible books – the Old Testament

1. *The Pentateuch (Books of the Law)* tell of the early days of the human race, the beginnings of the People of Israel, their escape from slavery in Egypt and the Laws they were to live by.

2. *Books of History* record the arrival in the 'Promised Land' of Israel; settling and living in the land and dealing with other nations in the area; their exile and eventual return from exile.

3. *Books of Poetry* are about people's reaction to God and each other. The Psalms are still used in Jewish and Christian worship today. The poetry doesn't rhyme as we understand it, even in the original Hebrew – but there is a rhyming of ideas between the parts of the verses.

4. *Books of Prophecy* are the words of prophets who proclaimed God's message to his people. The word 'prophecy' means 'messages about the future', but these books include many kinds of messages that God gave to his people.

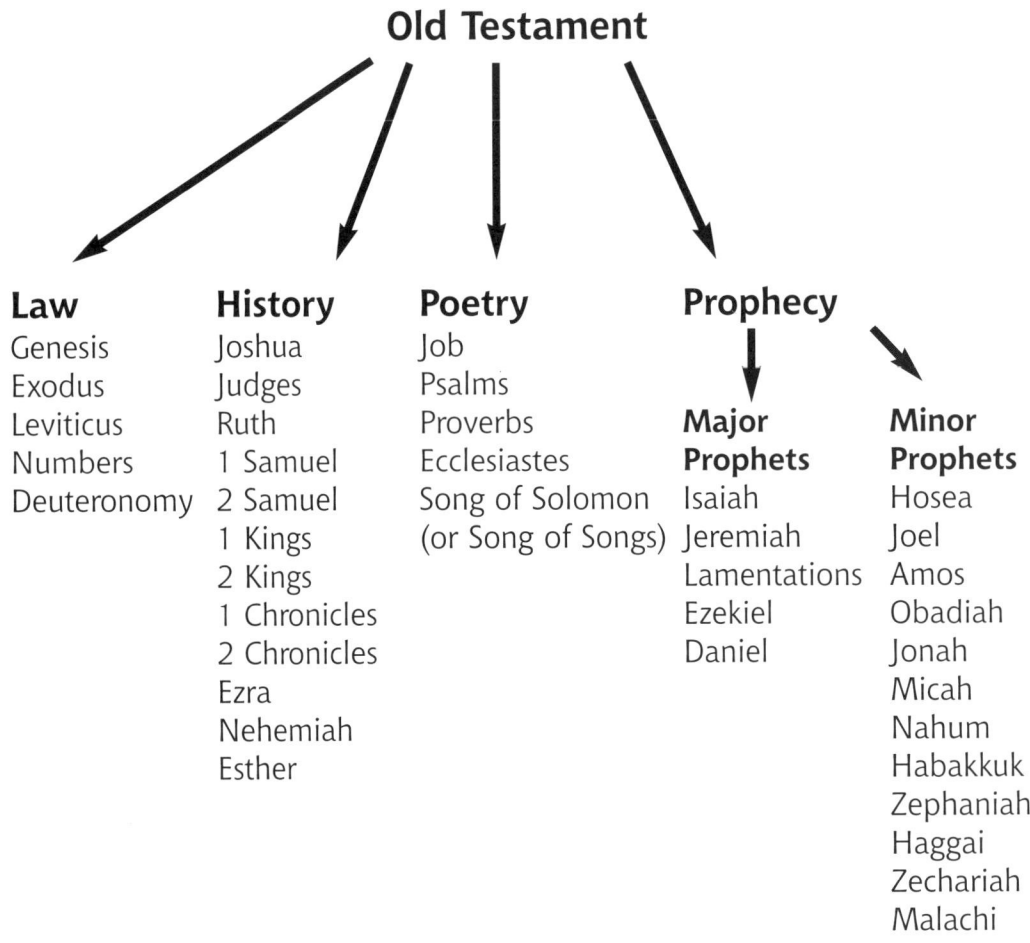

Old Testament

Law	**History**	**Poetry**	**Prophecy**	
			Major Prophets	**Minor Prophets**
Genesis	Joshua	Job	Isaiah	Hosea
Exodus	Judges	Psalms	Jeremiah	Joel
Leviticus	Ruth	Proverbs	Lamentations	Amos
Numbers	1 Samuel	Ecclesiastes	Ezekiel	Obadiah
Deuteronomy	2 Samuel	Song of Solomon	Daniel	Jonah
	1 Kings	(or Song of Songs)		Micah
	2 Kings			Nahum
	1 Chronicles			Habakkuk
	2 Chronicles			Zephaniah
	Ezra			Haggai
	Nehemiah			Zechariah
	Esther			Malachi

Bible books – the New Testament

1. *The Gospels* record the life, death and resurrection of Jesus.

2. *The Acts of the Apostles* tells how Christians, under God, took the Gospel about Jesus to many people in many places.

3. *Letters (Epistles)* were written by early Christians to individuals and to local churches.

4. *Revelation* is a vivid book of prophetic visions.

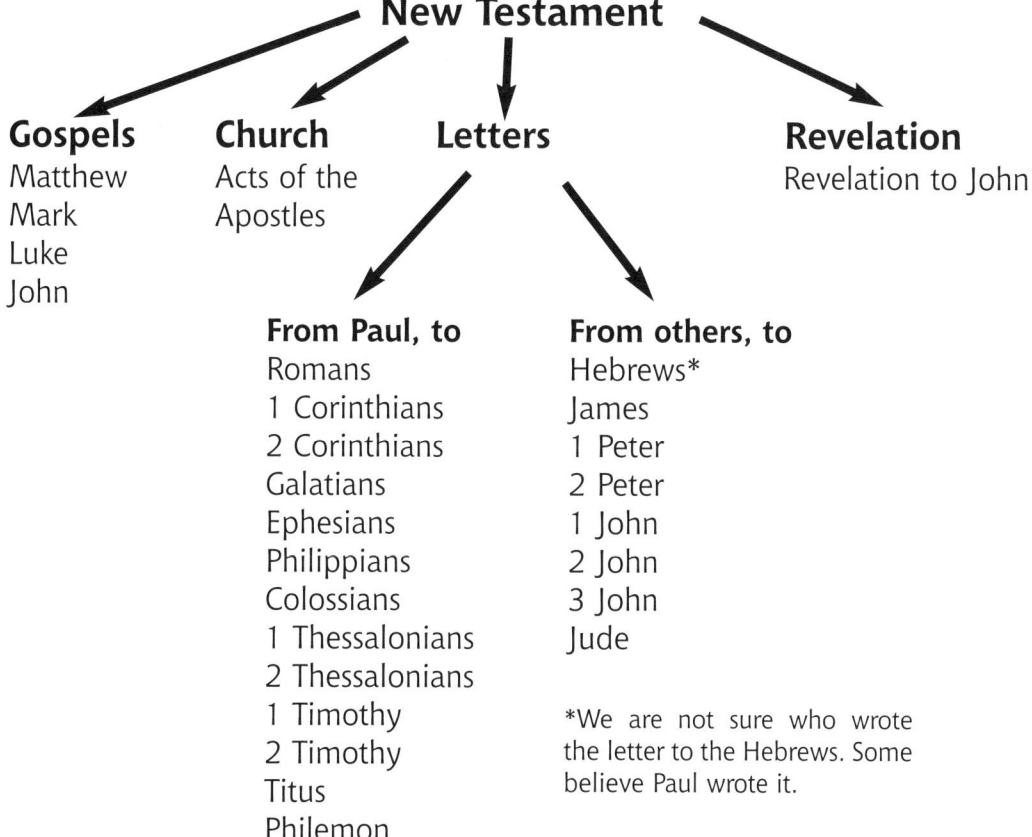

New Testament

Gospels
Matthew
Mark
Luke
John

Church
Acts of the Apostles

Letters

Revelation
Revelation to John

From Paul, to
Romans
1 Corinthians
2 Corinthians
Galatians
Ephesians
Philippians
Colossians
1 Thessalonians
2 Thessalonians
1 Timothy
2 Timothy
Titus
Philemon

From others, to
Hebrews*
James
1 Peter
2 Peter
1 John
2 John
3 John
Jude

*We are not sure who wrote the letter to the Hebrews. Some believe Paul wrote it.

Lesson Notes

These lessons are not necessarily to be taught in numerical order. Some lessons will specifically fit particular times in the Church Year, such as Christmas, and in these cases the suggested date is given in these notes.

Lesson 1: 'Who is God?'

The question 'Who is God?' is a question that most people ask at some stage in their lives. Although children will eventually come to different answers, it is right that they should be encouraged to consider what their answer should be, and to realise that there is a lot to be said for seriously considering religious answers. Many thousands of people have tried to answer the 'Who is God?' question over many centuries. Christians believe that we are unable to answer every question there is about God because of his greatness. At the same time God, who made us, is also concerned about us and wants us to understand more about him. The Bible is a record (Christians believe that it is *the* one inspired record) of God's dealing with mankind.

Much of our language comes from Latin, and three words stemming from Latin are used to describe God. He is described as *omnipotent*, meaning 'all-powerful', *omnipresent*, meaning 'in all places' and *omniscient*, meaning 'all-knowing'. These words describe the greatness of God, but they should be balanced by remembering that his love for his people overflows from the pages of the Bible.

The Bible verses on the reverse of the worksheets talk of some of the attributes of God. This can be attempted individually or by the class as a whole. The crossword asks questions about the attributes of God.

Lessons 2-4
Jesus' birth and early ministry

Suggested date for lessons – last week of November to the end of the Autumn term.

Christians believe that Jesus was not just a man, but the Son of God. He had no human father, although Joseph, who had plans to marry Jesus' mother, Mary, became his adopted father. The birth of Jesus (the 'Messiah' or anointed one) had been predicted in the Old Testament, yet the people expected him to be a mighty soldier rather than a leader of the thoughts and actions of people. They expected him to give them worldly power rather than the much greater gift of the possibility of having peace with God.

The fourth Sunday before Christmas (late November or early December) is known as Advent Sunday. The time up to Christmas Day (25 December) is the Advent period. In Advent, Christians generally think about three main issues: the proclamation and birth of Jesus; the return of Jesus; and the message of John the Baptist who prepared people to meet Jesus.

1. *The proclamation and birth of Jesus.* Prophets such as Isaiah talked about the birth of 'Immanuel', which means 'God with us' (Isaiah 7:14). He and other Old Testament prophets pointed forward to the one who was to come.

2. *The return of Jesus.* Luke 21:25-28 and other parts of the New Testament predict that Jesus will return as judge, taking his followers to be with him.

3. *The message of John the Baptist.* John predicted that the Messiah would appear, and told the people to repent in preparation for when he arrived. He baptised people by bathing them ritually in the River Jordan if they repented. (The word 'repent' means to admit your wrongdoing and seek to avoid repeating these faults.)

Lesson 2: The birth of Jesus

The first question is about how people should prepare for the return of Jesus. The answer is partly shown in Luke 21:25-28. People can be ready by trusting God and asking for his guidance in their lives; they will then have no fear about the future.

The next question is about a prediction of the coming of Jesus.

On the reverse of the worksheet is a crossword puzzle. The line under the arrow spells the word 'Christmas'.

The order of the pictures at the bottom of the page can be deduced by a careful reading of Luke 1:26-2:38. You may prefer to give a brief telling of that passage.

Lesson 3: Mary's hopes and fears

Mary was a tremendous person! She accepted the call of God, to be the mother of his Son, even though she thought that Joseph may abandon her and leave her to cope on her own. It will probably be worth having the Bible passages read aloud and then think of the emotions that Mary must have felt.

She must have had the usual joys and fears: concern about her own health and that of her child, concern about food, clothing, money to bring up the child. She would have had joy in looking forward to bringing up her child, thinking about how he would live and work and how she would be the best mother for her little one.

She would also have had thoughts about Jesus in particular: what kind of life would the Son of God lead? would he need any special upbringing? and could she be the best mother to bring him up? She would also have been joyful because she was doing what God wanted and that would be to everyone's benefit. She would love and enjoy her child.

Lesson 4: The message of John the Baptist

Today we have recognised ways of passing messages to many people. E-mail, radio, television and newspapers are just some of the ways that people use to influence lots of people. In biblical times things were not so simple. John the Baptist, the son of Elizabeth (Luke 1:34-38) was sent to proclaim that the Messiah was to come. John's clothing was rough and his preaching was very challenging. Luke 3:7-14 is printed on the reverse of the sheet with some words missing. The children are to consult the Bible and find the missing words. The vertical word under the arrow will show what John hoped would be the result of his preaching – 'righteousness'.

Lessons 5-11
Passover, Easter, Ascension and Pentecost

Suggested dates for lessons 5-9: second half of Spring term.
Suggested dates for lessons 10 and 11: about 5 to 6 weeks after Easter.

In this section we deal with the Christian celebration of Easter and the Jewish celebration of Passover. Both of these celebrations are celebrations of freedom and they are are very special to the people who faithfully take part. The two celebrations are linked because the death and resurrection of Jesus took place at Passover time, and his last supper was a Passover meal.

The Ascension was when Jesus returned to be with God, his heavenly Father; Pentecost, another great Jewish festival, was the day when the Holy Spirit was given by God to the followers of Jesus, making them able to be effective disciples.

Lesson 5: Exodus and the Passover

The word 'exodus' means 'going out', and the book of Exodus in the Bible tells of the people of Israel going out from slavery in Egypt.

The people of Israel had been slaves in Egypt for many years, but then Moses and Aaron were called by God to tackle Pharaoh, the King of Egypt, to lead the people away from Egypt and guide them back to their promised land of Israel. On the night they were to leave Egypt they were to have a special feast to celebrate their departure from slavery and to ensure that they would be well fed as they fled the land. Exodus 12 describes that event. If the children read verses 1-14 and 21-28 (together or individually), they will be able to put the events of the meal in the correct order.

Lesson 6: The Last Supper

Good Friday and Easter are special to Christians because Jesus, the Son of God, was prepared to be put to death for us but then defeated death by rising to life again. It was so special to Jesus that he gave a new meaning to the Passover festival for his followers as a mnemonic, or a way to help them remember what had happened.

(The mnemonic 'Men Very Easily Make Jugs Save Urns, Needles and Plants' is one I learned at primary school and I can still remember the order of planets from the sun because of it. Most people have some mnemonics that they remember, for instance 'Every Good Boy Deserves Fun' gives the ascending notes on the lines of a treble clef in music.)

Jesus gave bread and wine to the disciples (part of the Passover feast) to signify his death. His body (represented by bread) and his blood (represented by wine) would be given up for them (and those who would follow in their faith). The fullest description of the words of Jesus at the Last Supper are in 1 Corinthians 11:23-26, and these are used in the Holy Communion Service today, when Christians re-enact the Last Supper.

When Christians take Holy Communion they can have some or all of these thoughts and emotions: sorrow for their own sin, joy that Jesus was prepared to die to take their sins away, concern for other people (particularly those who do not know Jesus as their Saviour), feeling close to the Lord and enjoying togetherness with other Christians.

Lesson 7: Who is Jesus?

Jesus was unique in that he drew great crowds, even though his words were challenging and he had no worldly power-base and no access to modern communications. He made a number of great claims for himself, and used 'picture language technique'. He often described situations to help people understand about himself and God, his Father. The Bible verses on the reverse of the worksheet are about the ways Jesus described himself. The children are to find and write out these verses, then figure out which pictures on the front they are referring to.

Lesson 8: Crowds cheer Jesus

This lesson is about the actions of Jesus a week before he was crucified. Even though he was entering Jerusalem on an ass (perhaps the equivalent of a broken-down motor scooter), the people recognised him and made him a hero! It was mainly the religious hierarchy who felt that he was a threat to their privileges.

Lesson 9: Easter – the victory shown

The day Jesus was crucified is called 'Good Friday' by Christians. This must seem a strange title, because any crucifixion was a brutal, barbaric act. The crucifixion of Jesus was even worse! He was the Son of God and an innocent victim.

The day is known as 'Good', however, because of the results. It is good for us because Jesus' death can give us the freedom from sin that we all need. The Just One died for unjust people. Jesus was utterly right and holy – the only one who was right before God! His death was not because of his own sin but for ours, and because of his death we can be forgiven. The death of Jesus was no accident! It was the way that God the Father and his Son, Jesus, decided to save the world. Sin must be punished, but Jesus died to take that punishment.

Luke 24:13-19, 25-32 gives a description of one of the times that Jesus met the disciples after the crucifixion and the puzzle can be answered with the information in that passage from the Bible.

Lesson 10: The Ascension

Jesus had risen from the dead – and after that a number of things could have happened. First, he could have died a normal death – but as the Son of God, that would not have been the right thing for him. He had died once, and his rising had proved that he had conquered death.

Second, he could have just ceased to be there, but that would have left a lot of uncertainty with the disciples. Their proclamation of Jesus, if they ever decided to tell anyone about him, would have had a 'ragged' ending.

Third, Jesus could have stayed on earth, bound by human limitations. This would have been much less effective, as the disciples could not have 'gone out' to take his message to other people.

The fourth answer was one that nobody would have invented, but which was far better than human imagination could have concocted. Jesus made a miraculous 'ascension' to heaven. He had his disciples with him, he gave them some important messages, and he was lifted to the sky.

There were two main parts to the message. The first part of the message was that they should wait in Jerusalem until they were given the power to do their job. The second was that power would be given (see next week's notes on Pentecost).

Lesson 11: Pentecost

Jesus had been crucified at the feast of the Passover, and ascended forty days later. Pentecost was on the fiftieth day after Passover and most of the people were joining in this celebration, one of the Jewish Harvest Festivals. The disciples, however, were keeping themselves to themselves because they were frightened of being punished if they were seen to be followers of Jesus. They stayed in Jerusalem as they had been instructed when Jesus ascended.

Their shyness, however, was going to be instantly dissolved when they received the Holy Spirit. The Holy Spirit was the part of God which was alive in them and is still alive in Christians today, giving understanding about God's word and how he wants us to live.

The two main ways that the Holy Spirit works are through the 'fruit of the Spirit' (see Lesson 23) and the 'gifts of the Spirit' (1 Corinthians 12-14).

Lessons 12-15
How faith affects people

Part of the reason why many people avoid the Christian faith is the fact that they think of it as just strict 'do's and don'ts', without realising that real faith makes you joyfully try to do what is right. That is the way that these lessons should be prepared and taught.

Lesson 12: Baptism and Confirmation

Most organisations have some way of choosing and identifying their members. It may be a badge or clothing, like a school badge or a Scout uniform. People think of the Church as a strange shaped building, but in fact 'Church' really describes Christians who worship God through Jesus.

Baptism (a ritual washing) is the original sign of membership of the Church. John the Baptist originally baptised people to prepare them for meeting Jesus, and the Church took on baptism for when people became Christians. Soon Christians wanted all the family to be baptised, and the New Testament has examples of this happening.

There are two sets of questions which are asked at a baptism. These are entitled 'The decision' and 'The declaration of faith' on the back of the worksheet. In many Churches the baptism of children is acceptable, and these Churches have a later service so that older people can declare their faith in public. This is usually known as the Confirmation Service (where people confirm their faith) but other Churches have similar services with different names, such as the Methodists' Membership Service.

Lesson 13: Proclamation

The story on the front of the worksheet is a parable about a generous rich man who wanted to give to poorer people, but he was annoyed when one of these people didn't tell others about him. That is similar to God's way with us. We are invited to enjoy his love for us but we shouldn't be shy of telling other people about him. (See the last command of Jesus to his disciples in Matthew 28:16-20.)

On the back of the worksheet there is a question about other ways of proclaiming the message. Possible answers include: newspapers, radio, TV, Internet and books.

When the words are found in the wordsearch the remaining letters spell out a sentence.

Lesson 14: Loving action

The Bible reading is one of the Parables of Jesus. The story of the Good Samaritan would have been a shock to many of the faithful Jewish people, because the Samaritans were regarded by Jews as the lowest of the low. In past times the Samaritans had been unfaithful to God and worshipped idols. In Jesus' story a priest and a Levite, both respectable members of the community, walked past a man who needed help. The Samaritan was the one who went out of his way to help. (It is interesting to note that when Jesus asked which one acted as a neighbour, the Jewish lawyer didn't acknowledge the Samaritan, but described him as 'The one who was kind to him' (Luke 10:37).

The questions on the back of the worksheet are about our reaction to people who suffer and about crime prevention.

Lesson 15: Putting faith into practice

This lesson follows on from the last one. The first question is about the ways friends should behave towards each other, and the second about how we show that we love God. (Prayer and worship, enjoying his love for us, reflecting his love by kindness to others, etc.)

The back of the worksheet suggests various ways that young people can help others, and this can provoke useful discussion. It may be worth finding out what can be done locally and suggesting either that the class or some of them join in, or that the whole class start a useful project.

Lessons 16-19
Faith in action

Many people have the idea that religion is only for people who do not have any strength of character, and it is true that the Church is and should remain a refuge for those who find life difficult. However, the examples of the people in this section (and most Christians down the ages) show that faith and courage go together. In many cases of evil government throughout history it is Christians who have stood for what is right and proclaimed their faith in the most trying circumstances.

Lesson 16: Saint Paul

Paul was fiercely against the Christian Church at first. Acts 7:54-8:3; 9:1-2 tell of his bitterness against Christians and the way he tried to kill Christians and destroy the Christian faith. (Paul was originally called Saul.) However, when he was given a vision of Jesus his mind changed completely (Acts 9:3-25). He became the Christian faith's best missionary and he was prepared to face hardships which resulted from his firm Christian faith. (See 2 Corinthians 11:24-28, 12:10; Acts 27:13-44).

The wordsearch gives one of the results of Paul's work.

Lesson 17: Saint Francis of Assisi

Saint Francis is famous for his care for animals, but that is only a small part of his story. He had been a soldier and was a prisoner of war, but turned from the warlike way of life when he became a Christian. He started an Order of monks, the Franciscans, and did all he could to proclaim the Gospel. He died at just 44 years old, yet he had a great influence on many people down the ages.

Lesson 18: John Wesley

Although John Wesley was a clergyman, and tried very hard to do what was right, for a long time he failed to enjoy God's presence with him. He had started the 'Holy Club' in Oxford to do good works and even went as a missionary to American Indians, but only had a 'mechanical' faith and had no real joy in his heart. When he was returning from America the ship was in storms and nearly sank; John Wesley was terrified, but he was impressed by some German Moravian Christians who were calm and joyful through the ordeal. It was later, in a Moravian chapel in London, that he became a Christian and his heart was 'strangely warmed' as he knew God personally for the first time.

He spent the rest of his life in Great Britain, Ireland and America, joyfully telling people about the good news that he had discovered for himself.

Later, his followers started the Methodist Church to help people find out more about Jesus.

Lesson 19: Mother Teresa of Calcutta

Mother Teresa is one of the great saints of the twentieth century, even if she is not yet formally recognised as such. She had a living faith which gave her a determination to care for the people who were the poorest. Although she seemed a frail person, her achievements are huge. Her main work was in India, although she was born in Albania and lived in Ireland for a while.

Lessons 20-23
Rules and guidelines

Lesson 20: The Ten Commandments

The Ten Commandments were given by God to the people of Israel. Moses was given them, carved into stone. The people were travelling from Egypt where they had been slaves, towards the Promised Land. While in slavery they had had to do as they were told, but now that they had more freedom their actions had greater effect on the other people. The Commandments were given to make sure that people used their freedom in the best possible way, worshipping God and considering other people.

The puzzle on the front of the worksheet and the pictures on the back ask the children which Commandment each statement or picture refers to.

In the other puzzle the children are to pick the repeated letter in each tower of letters, and these letters will form a sentence.

Lesson 21: Jesus sums up the law

By the time of Jesus, the religious leaders had made religious observance and lawkeeping a very difficult job, and had removed the joy of being God's people. They had added all kinds of extra bits on to the Commandments and enjoyed catching people out if they made a mistake. When Jesus was asked a trick question he went down to the basics, and pointed to the need of love for God and your neighbour – if you got these things right everything else would follow.

In the puzzle on the back the children are to shade the drawing, putting a clear, dark colour in the sections containing a small circle. That will give Jesus' summary of the law.

Lesson 22: The Beatitudes

Some people in the time of Jesus – and in every age before or since – liked to keep themselves legally correct but then they acted wrongly towards God and other people. In his famous 'Sermon on the Mount', Jesus talked about the best way of life. He was not impressed by riches, and we shouldn't be either! Jesus was more concerned that love for God and people (see the previous lesson) should be uppermost in peoples' thoughts.

Jesus demonstrated this by giving the statements that are known as the Beatitudes. Some versions of the Bible talk about these people being 'blessed' but the translation 'happy' in the Good News Bible is a better one.

Lesson 23: The fruit of the Spirit

The Holy Spirit, a part of God, was given by the Father to Christians to guide their lives. Paul knew about the work of the Holy Spirit in his heart and life, and he realised that the Holy Spirit gave him lots of attributes which he described as the fruit of the Spirit. They are: love, joy, peace, patience, kindness, goodness, faithfulness, humility and self-control. In Galatians 5:16-23 Paul compares these with the kind of life which selfishness produces.

Lesson 1: Who is God?

This is one of the most important questions of all time, because people have been trying to answer it from the beginning of humanity. Our answer to this question affects how we try to travel our life's journey. If somebody asked you that question, how do you think that you would answer it?

_____

_____

_____

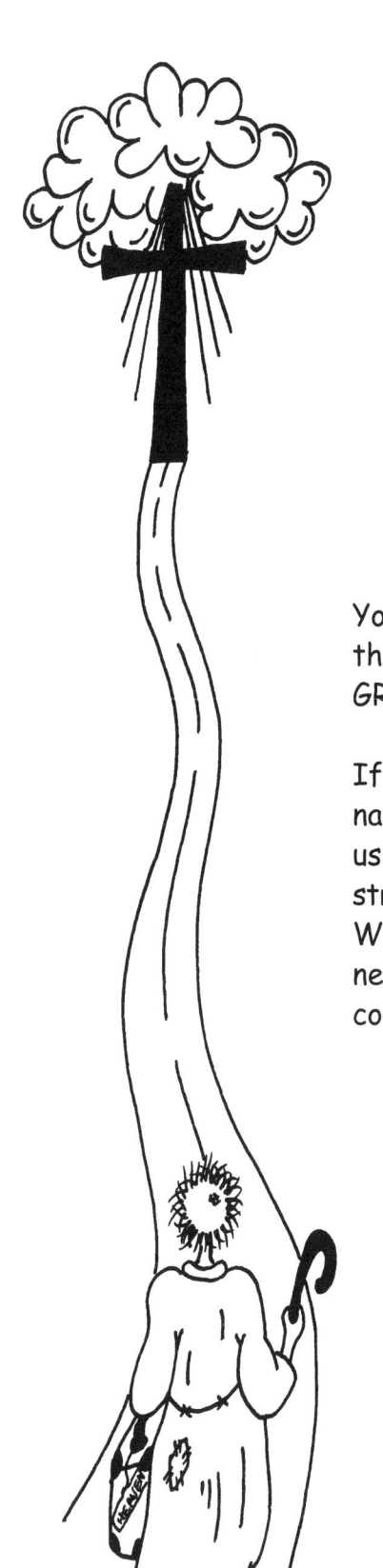

You cannot give an easy answer to that question, because of God's GREATNESS!

If you were talking about an ordinary person being great, you would usually be talking about one or two strengths or parts of his personality. When you talk about God's greatness, there are lots of things to consider.

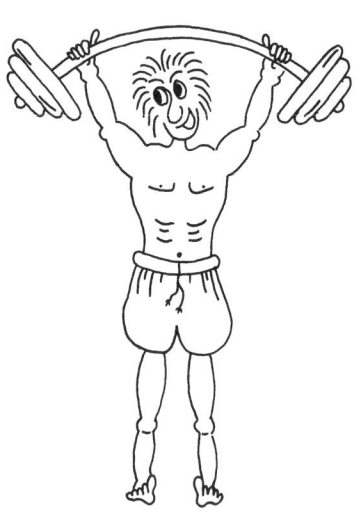

Omnes is a Latin word meaning 'all'. When we talk about God we are talking about one who is so great in every way that the words to describe him usually start 'omni' . . . because he is all-powerful and not just slightly powerful. Look at these 'omni' words for God, then look at the Bible verses and see which descriptions fit which words.

OMNIPOTENT . . . all-powerful
OMNIPRESENT . . . in all places
OMNISCIENT . . . all-knowing

He is also . . . all-loving

Read the Bible verses shown, and see if you can find the quality of God mentioned in those verses. Choose from: all-powerful; in all places; all-knowing; and all-loving.

Psalm 139:1-6 _____   Psalm 139:17-18 _____

Genesis 1:1-3 _____   Psalm 139:7-8 _____

Job 38:1-11 _____   1 Kings 8:27 _____

Matthew 24:37 _____   Revelation 1:4-6 _____

Crossword

Can you answer the clues? Hint – all these words are used to describe God.

Across
1 God is not just in heaven, but . . .
3 Like the man on the throne.
5 Strength.
6 God, or a ruler in this country.
7 Greatly caring for his people.
8 A person who cares for sheep.

Down
1 Never-ending.
2 The kind of power a king has.
3 Clever.
4 He makes all things.

Extra challenge

How many other words can you think of to describe God's greatness and his abilities?

Lesson 2: The birth of Jesus

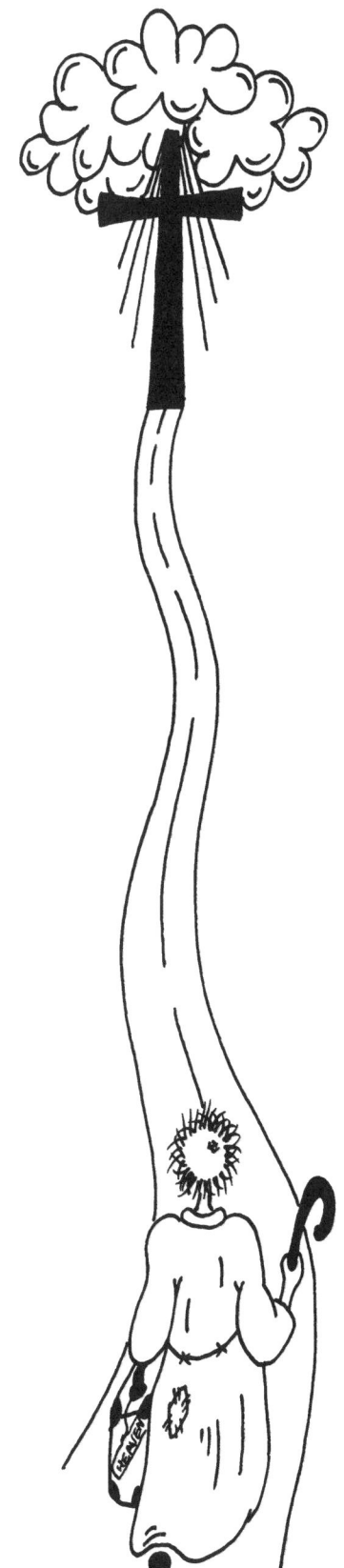

The word 'Advent' means coming, or approaching. If you are waiting for a special event it is important to you and you want to get ready for that event. The time of the birth of Jesus was something that a lot of people had waited for over many years!

The Jewish people had known more about God than anybody else, and they trusted his promises. They believed that he would send the Messiah to save the people.

Christians understand that Jesus *was* and *is* the Messiah. He came as a man, but also as the Son of God, to help people to understand about God.

When Jesus came to earth, he accepted human life with all its joys and pains. The most painful moments of his life on earth were caused by people not accepting him. To get the most out of our life's journey we should appreciate him.

The first appearance of Jesus was accurately predicted. In Advent we remember that during his time on earth Jesus told us that he would be returning to earth. Read Luke 21:25-28. How should Christian people approach that time?

If Jesus is coming again we should ask him to help us to be like him, so that we can receive him joyfully.

The time of Advent is about one month before Christmas. In that time we remember three things about Jesus:
1. The proclamation and birth of Jesus.
2. The return of Jesus.
3. John the Baptist preparing people to meet Jesus.

In the Bible, a prophet is a man who is given a special message from God for other people. Often this message was about something that would happen in the future. Prophets had spoken about Jesus for centuries!

Read what one of them said in Isaiah 7:14 and Matthew 1:23.

Quiz

Can you answer these questions? Put the answers in the boxes, and then find a word for a day in late December reading downwards. The Bible references are all from Luke's Gospel.

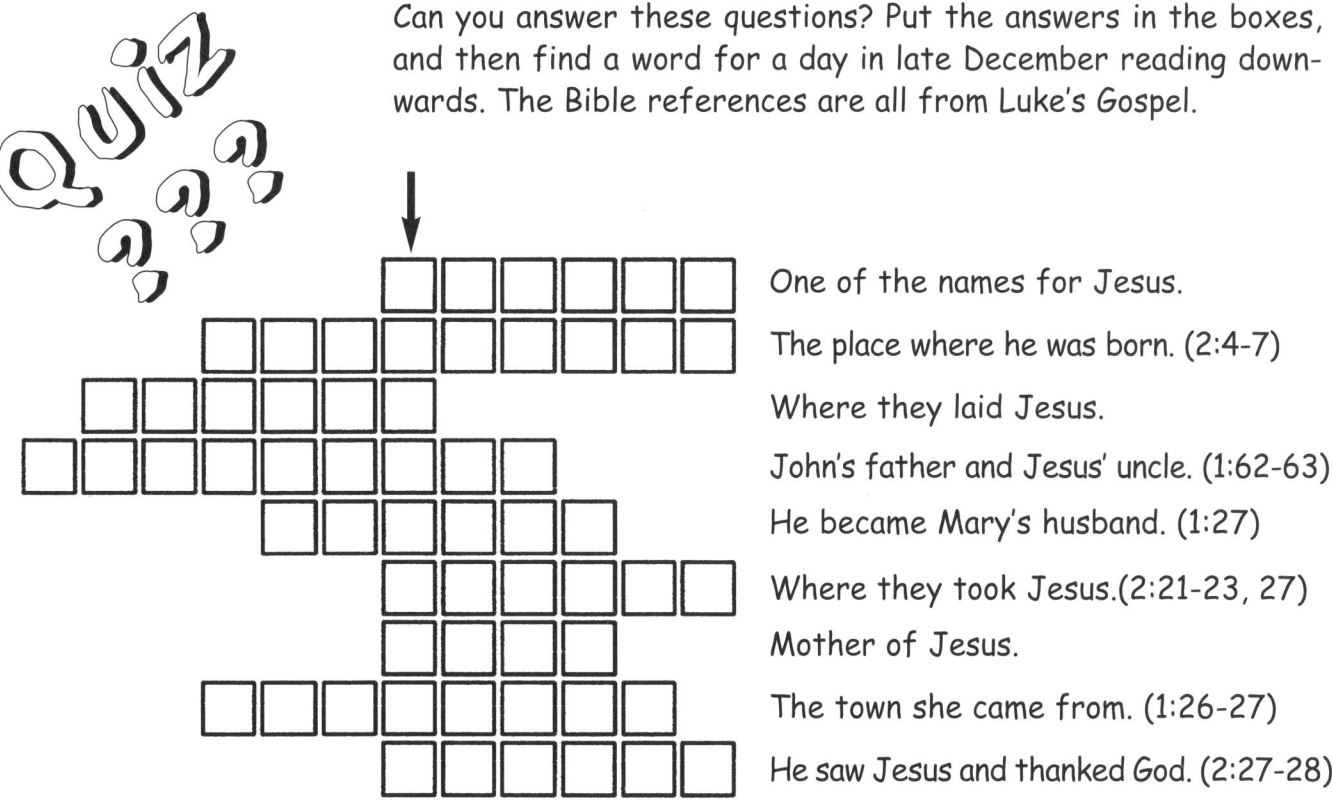

One of the names for Jesus.

The place where he was born. (2:4-7)

Where they laid Jesus.

John's father and Jesus' uncle. (1:62-63)

He became Mary's husband. (1:27)

Where they took Jesus. (2:21-23, 27)

Mother of Jesus.

The town she came from. (1:26-27)

He saw Jesus and thanked God. (2:27-28)

Number these pictures in the right order and colour them in

Extra challenge

Write about how you would prepare to meet someone very special.

Lesson 3
Mary's hopes and fears

When Mary was told that she would give birth to Jesus she must have had mixed feelings. She was a person who wanted to do what God asked, but she didn't want to have a fatherless child. Her life's journey would have been difficult.

Think what might have made her joyful and what would have made her worried.

Read Luke 1:26-38, 46-55

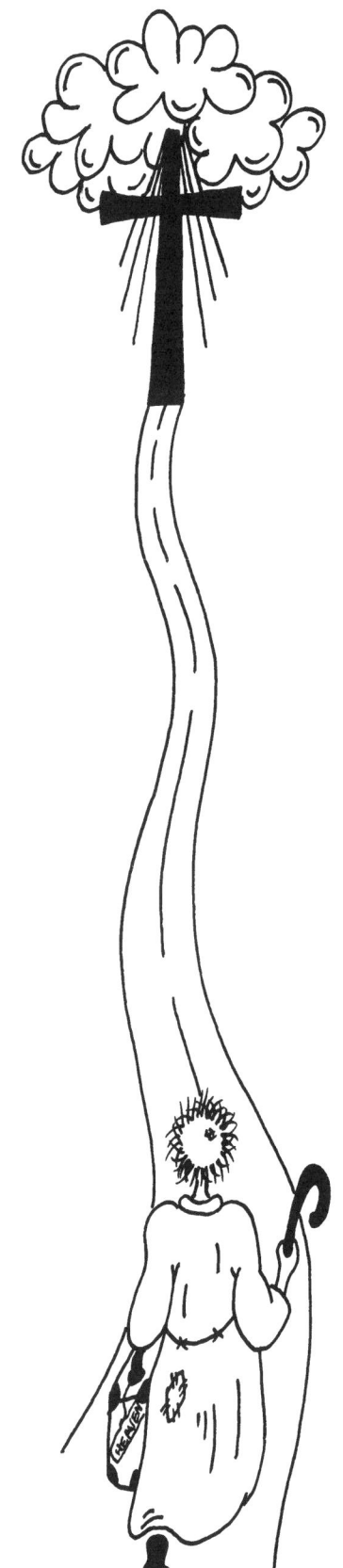

Why might she be frightened?

_____

_____

_____

Why was she happy?

_____

_____

_____

First
Find these words in the square and cross them out (they may be read forwards, backwards, up or down, but not diagonally).

Second
Copy the remaining letters into the grid to give a special message. Work from left to right along each row in turn.

Angel
Bethlehem
Elizabeth
Gabriel
Herod
Israel
Jesus
Joseph
Joy
Mary
Nazareth
Peace
Simeon
Song
Temple
Zechariah

E	L	I	Z	A	B	E	T	H	S	W	H
E	N	P	E	A	C	E	E	L	U	I	Z
A	B	E	C	T	H	M	E	T	S	M	A
B	E	T	H	L	E	H	E	M	E	R	Y
T	H	E	A	L	E	G	N	A	J	O	Y
L	E	A	R	S	I	H	E	R	O	D	Y
G	W	S	I	M	E	O	N	Y	S	E	R
N	A	Z	A	R	E	T	H	E	E	S	O
O	J	O	H	Y	F	T	E	M	P	L	E
S	U	G	A	B	R	I	E	L	H	L	!

_ _ _ _   _ _ _ _ _ _ _ _ _   _ _ _   _ _ _ _

_ _ _ _   _ _ _ _   _ _   _ _ _ _ _ _ _!

Use this space to draw a picture of Mary with the angel, or Mary thinking about her hopes and fears.

Extra challenge
Write about a time when you have been asked to do something special to help other people.

Lesson 4: John the Baptist and the hope of the people

If you wanted to give an important message to a lot of people, how would you do it?

_____

_____

_____

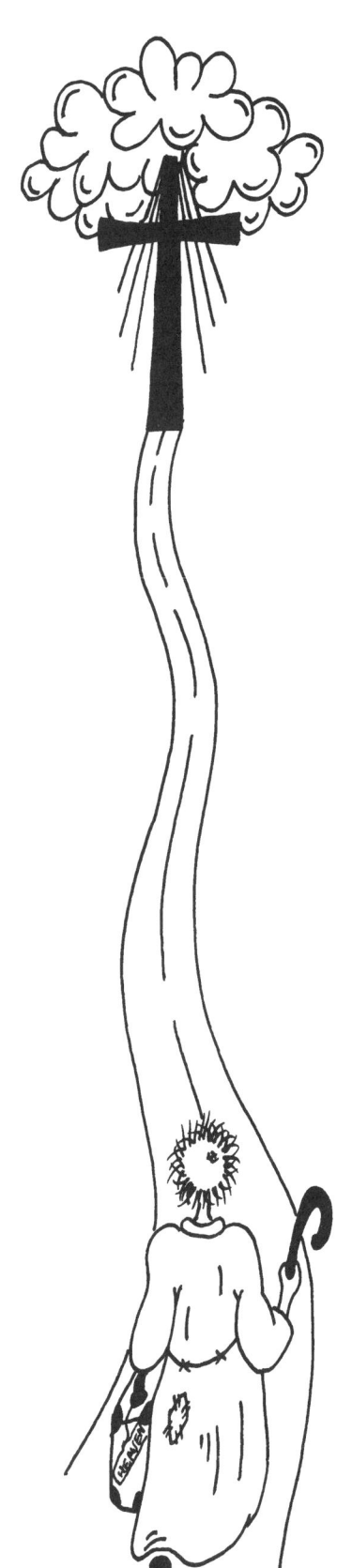

Today we are going to think about somebody who had an important message, but he probably worked very differently. God had promised a saviour to the Jewish people many years before Jesus actually arrived, although when he arrived they were expecting a very different kind of person! The kind of person they wanted would free the people from the Roman armies and give them the kind of power that the Romans then held.

Before Jesus started his work, his cousin, John the Baptist, was sent to the people to give them an idea about the kind of person they should expect. In a lot of ways John was a very different person to Jesus, but his message was an important one: to prepare the people to meet Jesus. Find out about him in Matthew 3.

Where did he live? (Verse 1)

_____

What did he eat? (Verse 4)

_____

What did he wear? (Verse 4)

_____

The things John said . . .

Because John said what was needed to help people to be ready for the Messiah, he didn't always say the things that they wanted to hear! Look on the back for a quiz about what he said to different people who lived in the area at the time. The answers can be found in Luke 3:7-14.

Quiz

In this quiz you find the missing words by looking at your Bible. The clue number is written after the word like this *1. Then transfer the words to the correct boxes, and see if you can follow the arrow and find the word reading downwards. Clue – the word is a word that John wanted the people to show.

(v 7) _ _ _ _ _ _ _*1 of people came out to John to be baptised by him. 'You _ _ _ _ _ _ _!' *10 he said to them. 'Who told you that you could _ _ _ _ _ _ *12 from the _ _ _ _ _ _ _ _ _ _ _*2 God is about to send? (v 8) Do those things that will show that you have _ _ _ _ _ _ *5 from your sins . . .'

(v 10) The people asked him, 'What are we to do then?' (v 11) He answered, 'Whoever has two _ _ _ _ _ _ _ *13 must give to the one who has none, and _ _ _ _ _ _ _ _ *4 has _ _ _ _ *7 _ _ _ _ *8 share it.'

(v 12) Some tax _ _ _ _ _ _ _-_ _ _ _ *11 came to be baptised, and they asked him, 'Teacher, what are we to do?' (v 13) 'Don't collect more than what is _ _ _ _ _ ',*3 he told them.

(v 14) Some soldiers also asked him, 'What about us? What are we to do?' He said to them, 'Don't take money from anyone by force or _ _ _ _ _ _ _ *9 anyone falsely. Be _ _ _ _ _ _ _*6 with your pay.

*1
*2
*3
*4
*5
*6
*7
*8
*9
*10
*11
*12
*13

What is the word that you are looking for?

_ _ _ _ _ _ _ _ _ _ _ _ _ _

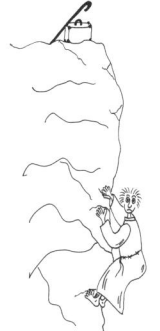

Extra challenge

What would a person like John the Baptist preach about today?

Lesson 5
Exodus and Passover

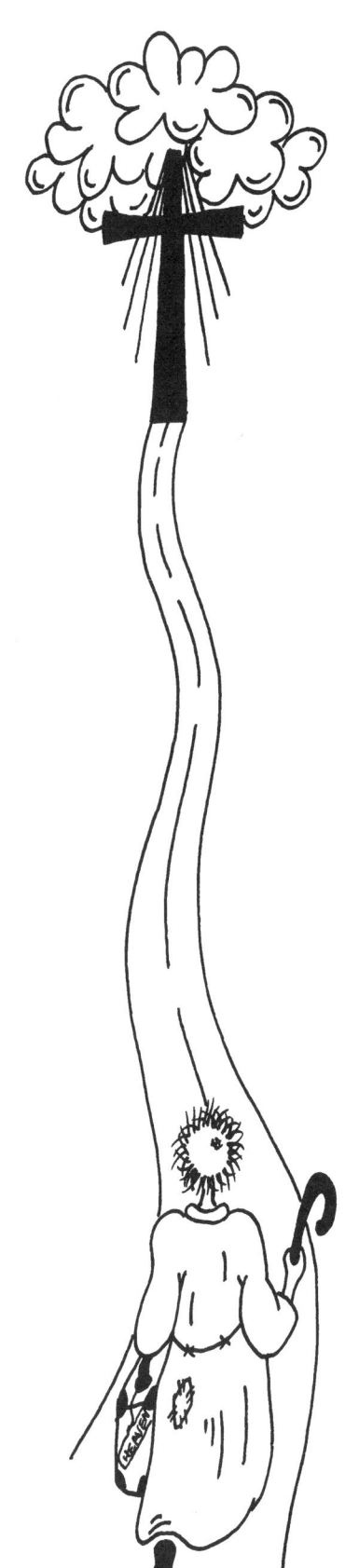

A special celebration for Jewish people is called 'Passover'. They celebrate the work of God in their nation long ago. They had gone to Egypt many years earlier as guests of the Egyptian people, but eventually they became slaves of the Egyptians. Do you remember the name of the man who was chosen by God to lead them out of slavery? – and what was his brother called?

- - - - - and - - - - -

This man had an exciting life's journey. He was frightened when he considered what he was being asked to do, as the Pharaoh (King of Egypt) was so powerful, but God let Moses take his brother along to help him. For a long time Pharaoh refused to let the people of Israel leave the land, even after promising to let them go, and God causing them problems when they refused. Eventually God decided to act more decisively! The oldest son of every Egyptian would die on the same night, and that would give the Israelites time to leave. These were God's instructions. Can you put them in the right order?

Read Exodus 12:1-14, 21-28

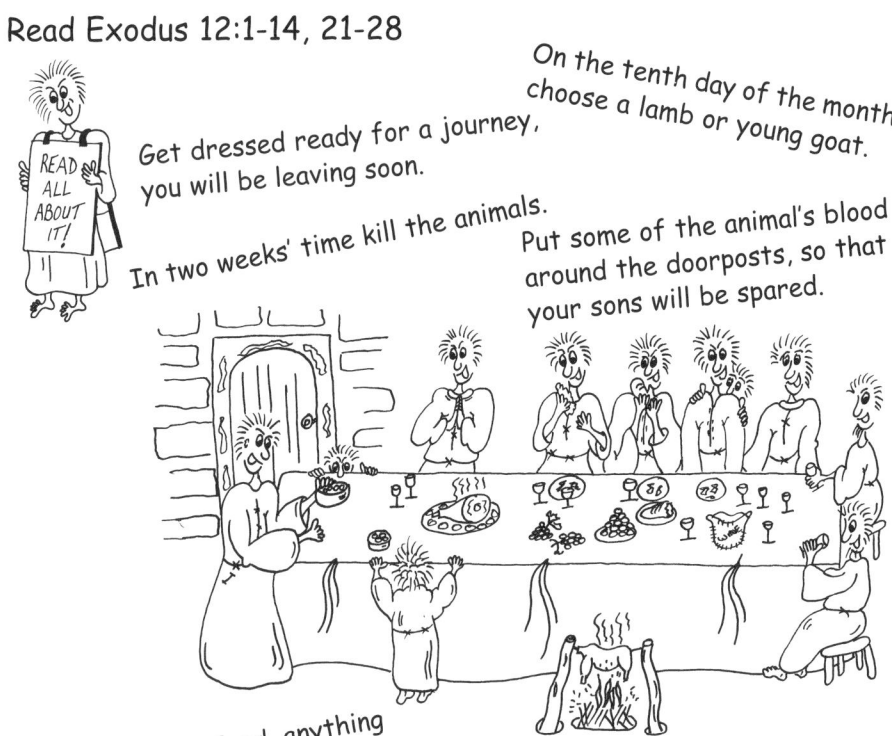

Get dressed ready for a journey, you will be leaving soon.

On the tenth day of the month choose a lamb or young goat.

In two weeks' time kill the animals.

Put some of the animal's blood around the doorposts, so that your sons will be spared.

Do not leave any food, anything uneaten must be burnt.

Do not leave the house until morning, then leave this land quickly.

Roast the meat and have a good feed, but eat it quickly.

Today will be New Year's Day for you.

The Passover was such an important event to the Jewish people that they still celebrate it today, more than three thousand years later. Next lesson we will see why it became an important event for Christians, and how they celebrate it.

Can you put these words into the grid? Hint – try the eight- and four-letter words first, and don't put any word in until you are sure it is the only one that will fit.

4 letters
Goat
Lamb

5 letters
Aaron
Egypt
Moses
Roast

6 letters
Israel
Travel

7 letters
Freedom
Pharaoh
Sandals

8 letters
Passover

9 letters
Celebrate
Doorposts
Sacrifice

Extra challenge

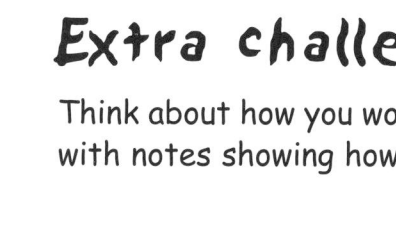

Think about how you would plan a very special celebration. Draw pictures with notes showing how you would do it.

Lesson 6: The Last Supper

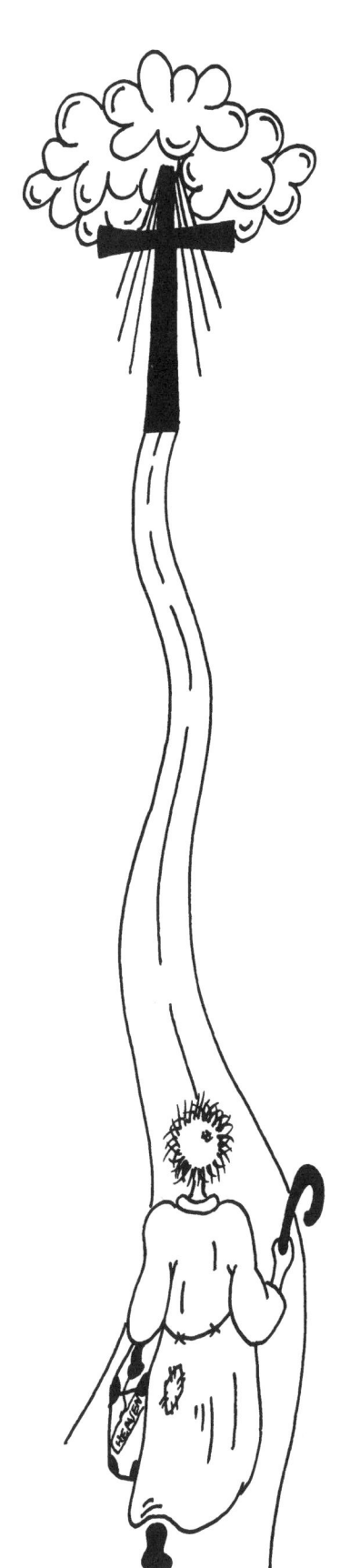

Men **V**ery **E**asily **M**ake **J**ugs **S**ave **U**rns, **N**eedles and **P**lants.
This sentence doesn't make much sense, but it is worth remembering, because it can help you to remember the names of the planets, starting from the nearest to the sun! The first two letters of each word are the same as the first two letters of a planet!
Mercury, **Ve**nus, **Ea**rth, **Ma**rs, **Ju**piter, **Sa**turn, **Ur**anus, **Ne**ptune and **Pl**uto.

Can you think of any surprising ways of remembering something important?

_____

_____

_____

Jesus often told stories and did unusual things to help people to understand important things about the work of God. Do you remember the last lesson, when we thought about the Jewish people celebrating the Passover? Jesus was crucified at the beginning of the Passover festival, and he ate the Passover meal with his disciples the evening before he was crucified.

There were several things about the meal that Jesus gave a new meaning to. He also told his followers to continue to take that meal as part of their life's journey. That is what we do when we have a Holy Communion Service in church. Jesus took bread and wine, using similar words to those used by Jewish people at every Passover meal – but he showed that he was the one who could save people from their sins.

The Passover lamb
The lamb was killed to nourish the people for their journey, so that they could safely leave Egypt and live in freedom. In the crucifixion Jesus was sacrificed for us, and he was described as the 'Lamb of God'.

Bread and wine
These were eaten as part of the feast. Jesus gave them a new meaning – to represent his body and blood which were given for his people. The good one died for the sins of the people. He told his followers to eat bread and drink wine together to remember his death for us, and this is what we do at Holy Communion Services.

1 Corinthians 11:23-26 describes the Last Supper, and these words are used in the Holy Communion Service in church today. What is the reason for the Holy Communion Service?

Can you find these words in the square?
(They may be read forwards, backwards, up or down, but not diagonally. Each word is in a different position on the grid, even if they are shown together on the list.)

Bread	Disciples	Meal
Body	Given	Passover
Blood shed	Holy Communion	Return
Dine	Last Supper	Wine

```
B L O S O V D B U N
C O M M U N I O N R
G B L O O D N D W U
I X S L U L E Y I T
V M U N K A H O N E
E L P A S S O V E R
N O P I C T L M I M
B R E A D L Y E L I
O N R D E H S A D N
A D I S C I P L E S
```

Extra challenge

Can you think how Christians might feel when they take Holy Communion? Write and explain your answer.

Lesson 7: Who is Jesus?

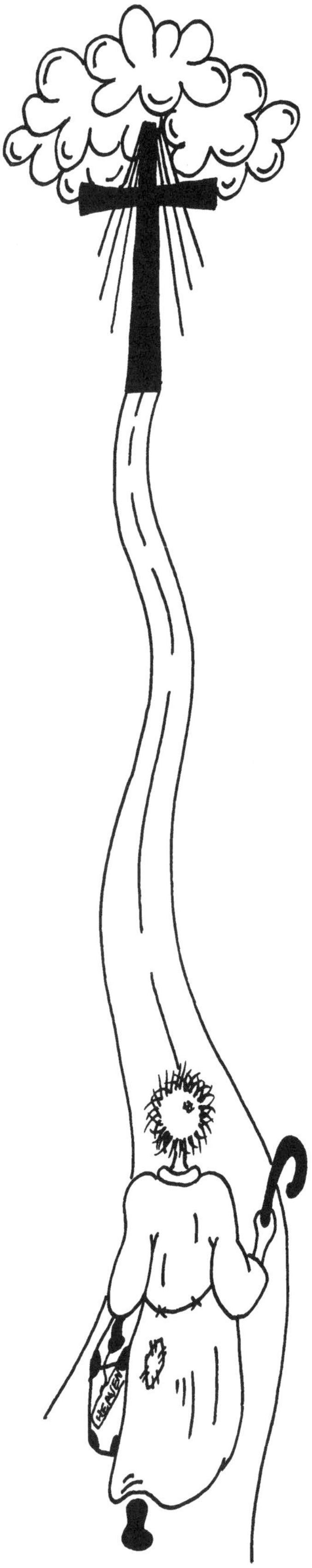

Can you think of any great, living person that you wish to be like? Say who, and why.

_____
_____
_____
_____

Lots of people have done great things, and people attract followers for good reasons and for bad ones! Jesus had some followers in his lifetime and still has many today – but people appreciate Jesus for all the best reasons. The names that Jesus was given and that he called himself give us a lot of clues why he is so special.

Quiz ???

Look at these pictures, then look overleaf to find some of the names for Jesus from your Bible. Then say which picture fits with which verse.

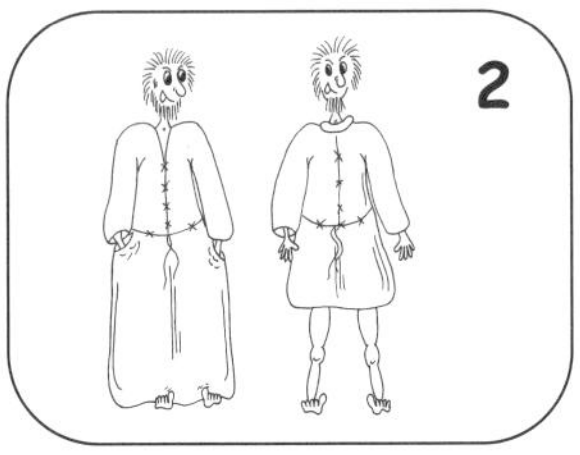

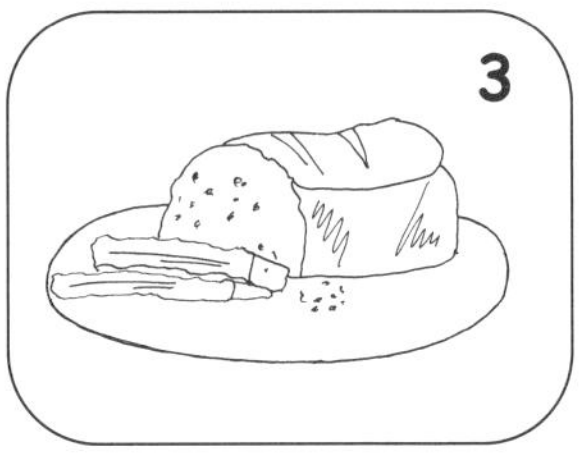

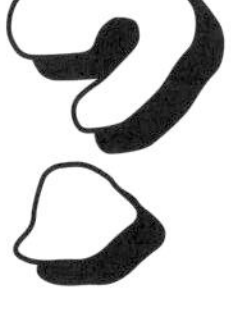

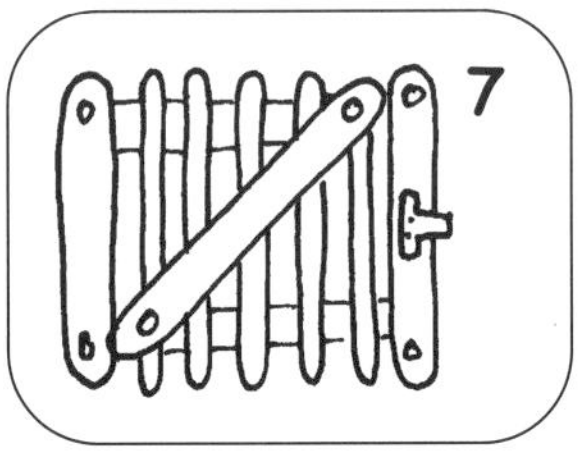

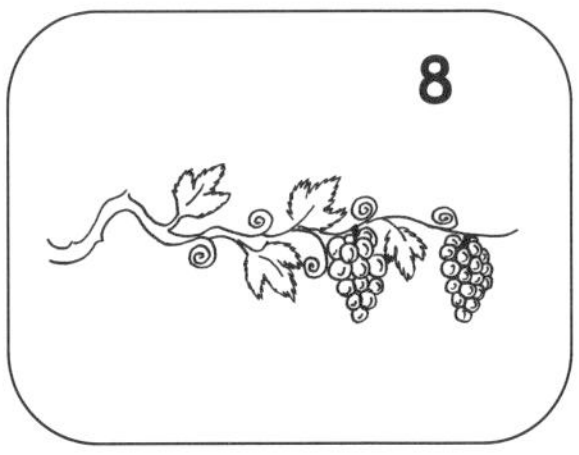

1. [candle]
2. [two people]
3. [bread]
4. [mountain/rock]
5. [classroom - Year 6]
6. [sheep]
7. [gate]
8. [vine with grapes]

John saw Jesus coming towards him and said, 'There is the _ _ _ _ _ _ _ _ _ who takes away the sin of the world.' (John 1:29) Picture ____

Jesus said, 'I am the _ _ _ _ _ _ _ _ _ _ _ _ _ _ _ _ _.' (John 8:12) Picture ____

Descriptions which help us to understand who JESUS is and the work he did.

Jesus said, 'I am the _ _ _ _ _ for the sheep.' (John 10:7) Picture ____

Jesus said, 'I am the _ _ _ _ _ _ _ _ _ _ _ _ _.' (John 6:35) Picture ____

Nicodemus said, 'Rabbi, we know you are a _ _ _ _ _ _ _ _ sent by God.' (John 3:2) Picture ____

Jesus said, 'I am the _ _ _ _ and you are the branches.' (John 15:5) Picture ____

What the Father does, the _ _ _ also does. (John 5:19) Picture ____

You will call him Jesus, because he will _. (Matthew 1:21) Picture ____

Extra challenge

Pick one or two of these descriptions of Jesus. Say why Jesus used this description. Draw a picture to illustrate the answer.

Lesson 8
Crowds cheer Jesus!

A football team that won the cup . . .
would travel round its home town on an open-topped bus to show off the cup.

A famous pop group . . .
would hire a football stadium and be seen by thousands of fans.

A member of the royal family . . .
would travel in a luxury car or (on special occasions) a horse-drawn coach.

When he was approaching his most important moment **Jesus travelled on a donkey!**

Jesus was approaching Jerusalem in his final week before the crucifixion. He knew what would happen, but at the time nobody else knew.
 Jesus was facing the most difficult part of his life's journey. Many people, including the rulers, were going to turn against him and he would be crucified. On Palm Sunday, however, Jesus was going to be made their hero.

Read Luke 19:28-40, then go to the next page and try to answer the questions.

1. Jesus told the disciples to untie something. What was it? _____

2. How often had it been ridden? _____

3. When they untied the donkey, somebody complained, but they said what Jesus had told them to say. What was it? _____

4. What was used as a saddle? _____

5. A crowd of people appeared. What kind of people? _____

6. What did they throw on the road? _____

7. What did they shout? _____

It was a pity that their voice could not be heard the following week when the authorities turned against Jesus, but God's plan triumphed anyway!

Draw a picture to show how you think Jesus' procession may have looked.

Extra challenge

Why do you think that everyone cheered Jesus?

Lesson 9
Easter – the victory shown!

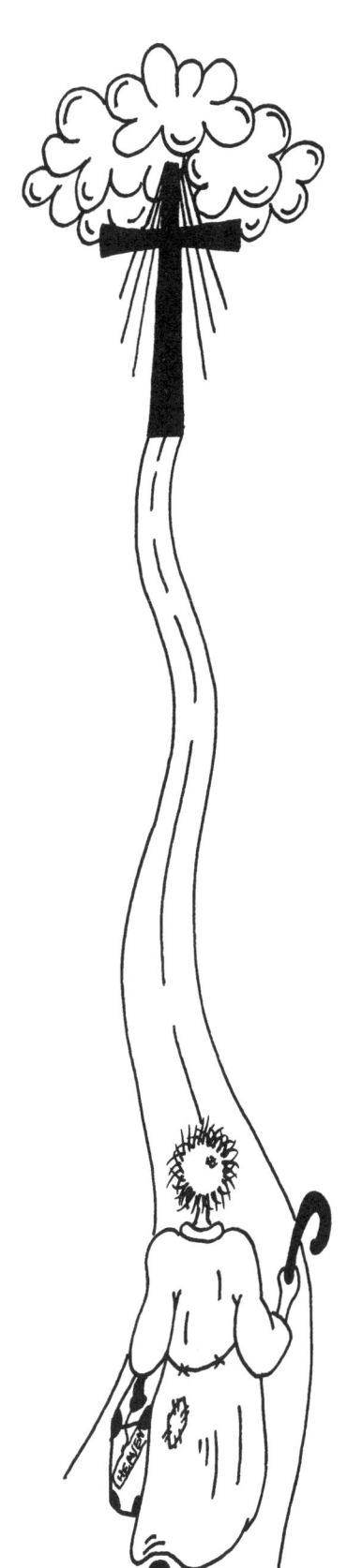

Jesus was cruelly put to death on the Friday of the Passover Festival. What do Christians call that day? _____

It must seem a very strange name for the day when God's Son was put on the cross. However, it is only 'Good' when you consider some of the other facts about that day, in particular:

Jesus died so that we could be forgiven. When he died, he took the shame that we should carry.

Jesus conquered death!!

The followers of Jesus certainly didn't expect him to rise from death. They had expected him to show his power to prevent himself from being crucified, but when they knew that he had died on the cross they thought that must be the end. **They were wrong!**

The Bible tells us several things that Jesus said and did after he had risen from death. But how do we know that it is true? The best way is to consider how the disciples changed. They were timid, frightened men before Jesus was crucified. After he had risen they told everyone, even though some of them were put to death for doing so! They had seen Jesus conquer death – so now it held no fears for them.

In Luke 24:13-19, 25-32 you can read about one of the times when Jesus was seen after he had risen.

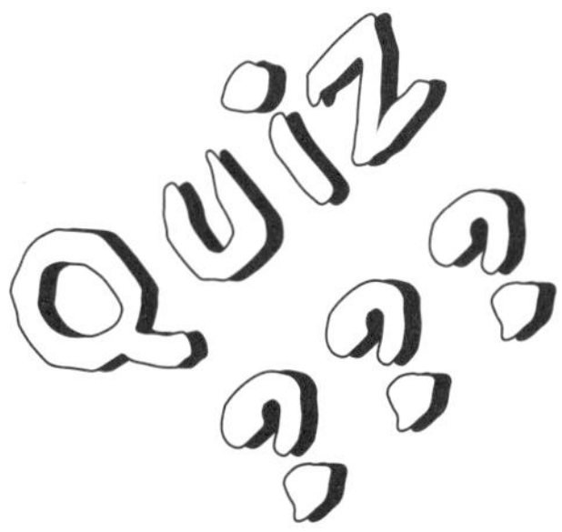

Quiz

Try to find the missing words in this quiz. Carefully read the Bible passage and then try to answer the clues. When the words are placed in the correct boxes you will be able to follow the arrow and find a sentence reading downwards. Clue: the sentence tells of the disciples' joyful surprise.

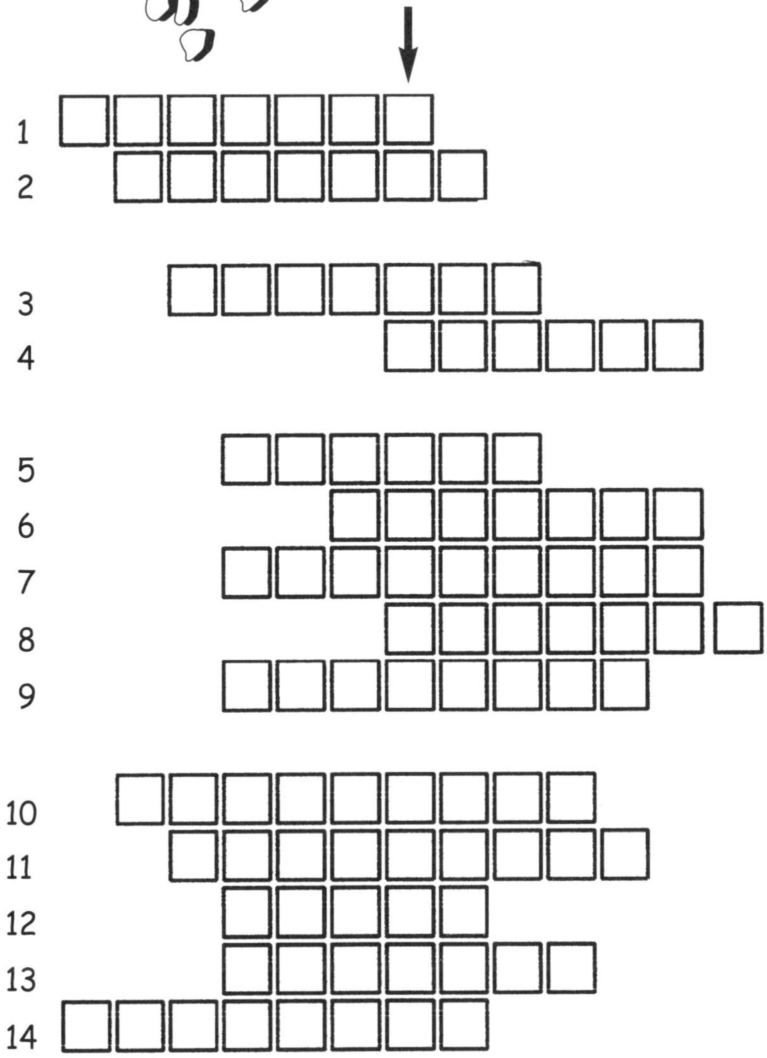

1. The one the prophets talked about in the past. (v 26)
2. Somebody who tells a message from God. (v 19)
3. This kind of person makes mistakes because he is not very wise. (v 25)
4. Jesus did this when he was on the cross. (v 26)
5. Where the disciples were going. (v 13)
6. The name of one of those disciples. (v 18)
7. Another word meaning the Bible. (v 27)
8. Emmaus was a _____. (v 28)
9. Jesus had shown that he was _____. (v 19)
10. The place where the people had started to walk. (v 13)
11. Eventually they were able to _____ Jesus. (v 31)
12. Jesus took this and broke it. (v 30)
13. They thought that Jesus was a _____ to the area. (v 18)
14. Jesus gave this just before he left them. (v 30)

The sentence is . . .

__ __ _____ _____!'

Extra challenge

Why do you think that this victory was much greater than a sporting or military victory? Draw a picture of the expressions on the disciples' faces when they saw that Jesus had risen.

Lesson 10: Ascension

When an aeroplane or a bird takes off or flies higher it ascends.

When you go up in a lift you ascend.

When you jump high you ascend.

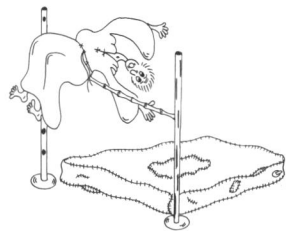

A special time of celebration for Christians is Ascension Day. Like most of the other great Christian festivals it commemorates something about the life of Jesus and reminds us of things we should know about him. After Jesus had died and risen he was going to return to God, the Father, yet he wasn't going to die again. How do you think he left the earth?

_____

_____

Now see what the Bible says: read Luke 24:45-53 and see what actually happened forty days after that first Easter.

What had to happen before Jesus died? (v 46)

_____

What happened next?

_____

What would the disciples (and future Christians) have to do? (v 47)

_____

The disciples didn't see Jesus after that. Where did he go? (v 51)

_____

First find these words in the arrow and cross them out. (They may be read forwards, backwards, up or down, but not diagonally.)

    Ascended
    Disciples
    Jesus
    Judea
    Lands
    Message
    World

Then copy the remaining letters into the grid below to give a special message. Work from left to right along each row in turn.

__ ____ __ __ _____

_ ____ ____ ___

____ ___ _____.

What would the ascension of Jesus have looked like? Draw your ideas.

Extra challenge

Do you think it is important that the disciples saw Jesus ascend from the earth? Why?

Lesson 11: Pentecost

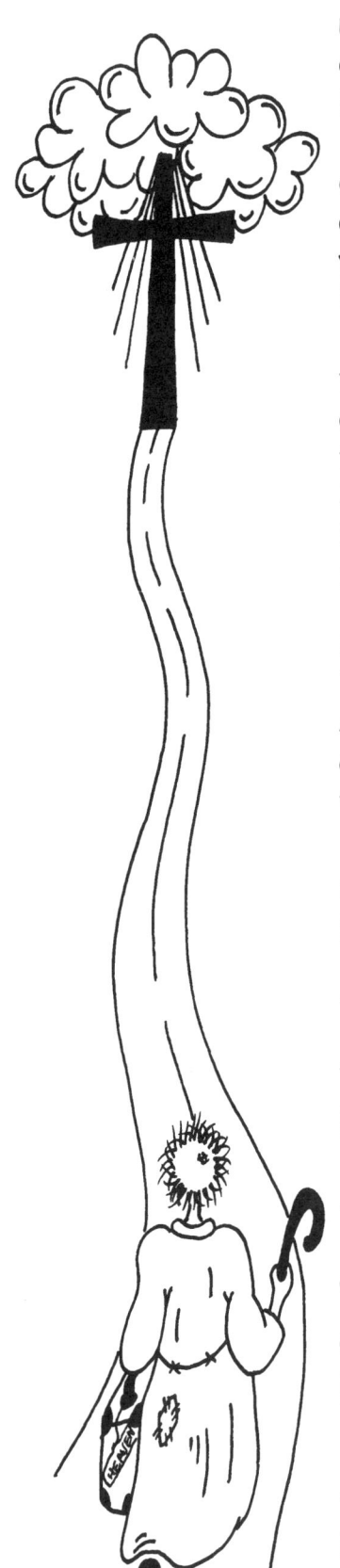

The followers of Jesus were a very frightened group of people. The same people who put Jesus to death may have wanted to turn on them! They had been delighted when Jesus rose from death, but now he had left them again. It was Pentecost time, and while most of the people were having a good time, the disciples of Jesus were keeping themselves hidden.

For the Jewish people the day of Pentecost was a very special event. In churches in this country we enjoy harvest festivals in the autumn, but the Jewish people have *two* harvest festivals each year. Pentecost is a festival earlier in the year when wheat is harvested.

Pentecost is fifty days after the feast of Passover, which is the time of year when Jesus was crucified. Jesus ascended forty days after that, so the Pentecost festival was just over a week later. At the big feasts of the Jewish faith there were many people in Jerusalem, and so Jerusalem was very crowded. The disciples were in the same upstairs room where Jesus had celebrated the Last Supper when something strange happened to them.

Read Acts 2:1-8
Those disciples who had been shy of meeting people suddenly started to tell the world about Jesus! Their fear had gone and nothing could stop them! What were the amazing things that happened to them?

A n_ _ _ _ from the s_ _ like a s_ _ _ _ _ _ w_ _ _ _.
(v 2)

They saw t_ _ _ _ _ _ _ of f_ _ _ which spread out and t_ _ _ _ _ _ _ e_ _ _ p_ _ _ _ _ _ t_ _ _ _.
(v 3)

They were f_ _ _ _ _ _ with the H_ _ _ _ S_ _ _ _ _ _ and began to s_ _ _ _ in other l_ _ _ _ _ _ _ _ _ as the Spirit enabled them to speak.
(v 4)

These were really strange events, but God wanted to make it known that this was to be the birth of the Church and it was really special. It got other people to rush to see what was happening, and so three thousand people became Christians on that one day.

Anny's language

Cannyan yannyou dannyo thannyis?
Mannyost cannyannot.
Onannyly clannyever peoannyple cannyan.

Like most languages, this looks impossible to anyone who does not know the language. In this case, however, it is quite simple! If you write the words down, but leave out the letters 'anny' where they appear together you can see a simple message in English.

Anny's languge is quite simple, and almost anyone can use it for fun, or even develop their own language! When the Holy Spirit gave words to the disciples, however, they weren't just using an 'anny' type of language.

Some people have the gift of being able to speak in strange languages, but the disciples were people who had never travelled beyond the area between Galilee and Jerusalem. The Holy Spirit was given at that Pentecost festival to help the disciples in the job they had been given. Jesus had promised that the Holy Spirit would be given, but the disciples didn't know what to expect. When the Holy Spirit came he enabled them to be very effective in the service of God.

1. They were using real languages.
2. The languages were from many lands.
3. Those lands were far apart.
4. The disciples had never spoken to people who used some of those languages.
5. The listeners understood them!

This message is written in the 'Ji' language which is constructed in the same way as the 'Anny' language. Can you work out what it is saying?

Theji Hojily Spijirijit wajis gijivejin soji thajit theji fojillowjiers jiof Jesujis wejire ajible jito stojip bejiing frighjitejind ofji adjimijitting thajit thjieyji wejire Chrijistijians, anjid thjieyji starjited jito tejill peojiple ajiboujit hijim, soji soojin therjie wejire majiny whoji joijinjied thejim.

_____
_____
_____

Extra challenge

The Bible talks about several 'gifts of the Spirit', and speaking in strange languages is one of them. Can you find any others in 1 Corinthians 12-14?

Lesson 12
Baptism and Confirmation

Think of a group or organisation that you belong to. It can be a Church uniformed organisation, your school, a band, a sports club or any other sort of organisation.

What is the organisation called? _____

What does it do? _____

How do you become a member? _____

Draw a sketch of the badge.

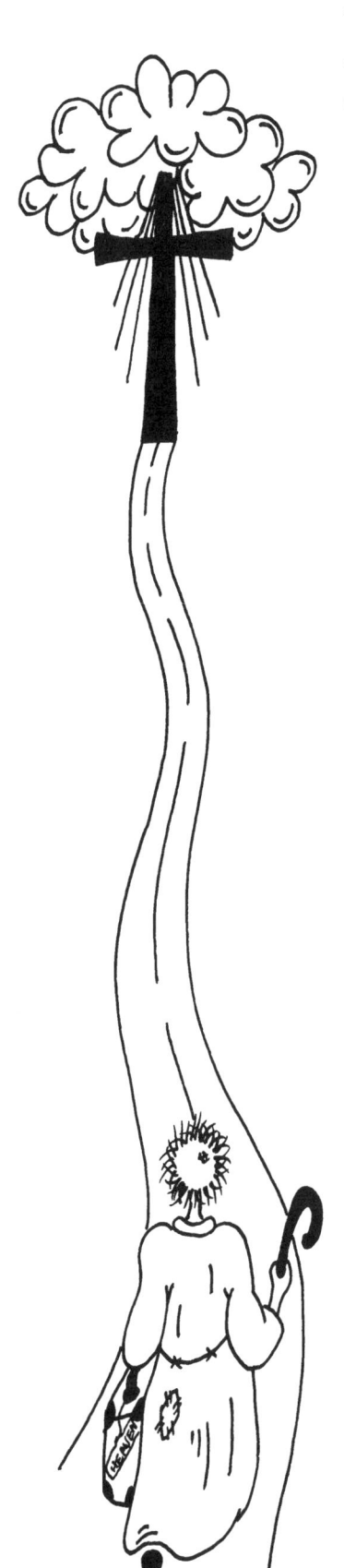

The Church has many fine buildings, although the Church is not the buildings but the people! It has many members throughout the world – yet how do we signify church membership? We believe that God wants everyone to follow him (though we all have the choice of accepting or rejecting him and many people reject him).

In Baptism we see God's acceptance and our response, and the one being baptised is washed, to represent the washing away of sins. It is meant to be the start of the Christian part of our life's journey. The godparents declare their faith, praying that a child will eventually come to a living faith himself or herself. Often people are baptised when they are older if they become Christians but were not baptised when they were young.

In Confirmation people make a declaration of faith for themselves, and are accepted as full members of the Church.

Do you know? What questions are asked at Baptism and Confirmation Services? Answer on the back!

In a children's or babies' Baptism Service the parents and godparents promise that they will help the young ones to grow up in the family of the Church with their help and by their example and teaching. Apart from that the questions are the same in Baptism and Confirmation. They are in two sections, 'The decision' and 'The declaration of faith'.

These questions are of vital importance. However, we must realise that answering the questions in a church service can be a lie if they are said without a real desire to let God be at work in our lives and so grow nearer to him each day.

The decision:

Question: Do you turn to Christ?
Answer: *I turn to Christ.*
Question: Do you repent of your sins?
Answer: *I repent of my sins.*
Question: Do you renounce evil?
Answer: *I renounce evil.*

The declaration of faith:

Question: Do you believe and trust in God the Father, who made the world?
Answer: *I believe and trust in him.*
Question: Do you believe and trust in his Son, Jesus Christ, who redeemed mankind?
Answer: *I believe and trust in him.*
Question: Do you believe and trust in his Holy Spirit, who gives life to the people of God?
Answer: *I believe and trust in him.*

Draw a picture of the Baptism of a child

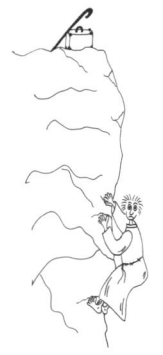

Extra challenge

What kind of things can parents and godparents do to help children grow in the Christian faith? Does their way of life affect their ability to do this?

Lesson 13: Proclamation

Imagine that Mr and Mrs Sopoor were very poor and their house was falling to pieces. The wooden window frames were rotting. Slates had fallen off the roof and rain came in. They could never afford to have a proper meal for themselves or the children. They lived in a land where people had to pay doctors' fees and so they couldn't get any medical treatment.

Mr Eimrich in the next town was very well-off, and he often helped poor families by giving them money and paying for repairs. One day he heard about the Sopoors and he decided to help. The Skint family lived near him, and he had often helped them, so he asked Mr Skint to go and see the Sopoors and tell them to visit Mr Eimrich so that they could tell him what was needed. Mr Skint didn't bother, he was too mean!

Draw a picture showing how Mr Eimrich must have felt.

Read Matthew 28:16-20
If we are Christians, God is like Mr Eimrich to us! He doesn't pay every bill, but he does so much more! He wants us to know forgiveness and new life. As we travel life's journey he wants us to have the joy of knowing that we are right with him, and he wants us to let him guide our lives. He wants us to live our lives to please him and he wants other people to share in the joy of knowing him.

The Bible passage we have read is a very important one. It tells us the last things that Jesus said before he returned to heaven. In your own words, what was the command he gave to Christian people?

_____

_____

If we appreciate our life's journey with Jesus we will want to tell everyone about it, but how do we do that? One way is shown in the picture on the left, another is preaching in church – but there are many other ways. Can you think of any?

_____

_____

The word 'Gospel' means 'Good News'. The early Christians knew that when they told people about the Gospel it really was [and still is] Good News. It is worthwhile trying to understand it and tell other people about it.

In different places at different times people were prepared to face danger when others turned against the Gospel, because it was so important to them to do what Jesus told them to.

There is a group of people who call themselves the Gideons. They want the Bible to be available to as many people as possible and so they pay to give Bibles to secondary schools, nurses' homes, hotels, prisons and many other places. That is how they preach the Gospel.

The Bible has been translated into hundreds of different languages so that as many people as possible can read it.

First find these words in the square and cross them out. (They may read forwards, backwards, up or down but not diagonally.)

Bible
Good News
Proclaim Gospel*
Gideons
Send
Into
World

L	E	P	T	S	U	S	T	R	Y	T
O	G	R	U	E	N	D	E	R	S	T
G	O	O	D	N	E	W	S	A	N	D
G	S	C	O	D	L	R	O	W	D	S
W	P	L	O	R	B	D	A	N	I	D
S	E	A	P	G	I	D	E	O	N	S
E	L	I	A	K	B	A	B	O	T	U
T	H	M	I	S	W	O	R	K	O	.

* In different positions on the grid.

Then copy the remaining letters into the grid below to give a special message. Work from left to right along each row in turn.

_ _ _ _ _ _ _ _ _ _ _ _ _ _ _ _ _ _ _ _ _ _ _ _

_ _ _ _ _ _ _ _ _ _ _ _ _ _ _ _ _ _ _ _ _ _ _ _ .

Extra challenge

Do you know how many books there are in the two parts of the Bible? Do you know some of the the kinds of writing in them?

Lesson 14: Loving action

Often Jesus told stories (or parables) to help people understand more about how they should live on life's journey. One of the stories was about a man who went on a journey.

Read Luke 10:29-37

This is an amazing story, because the Jews and the Samaritans hated each other! Jesus, a Jew, told the story, yet the star of the story was a Samaritan! See what the Bible says, then put the pictures in the correct order and colour them in.

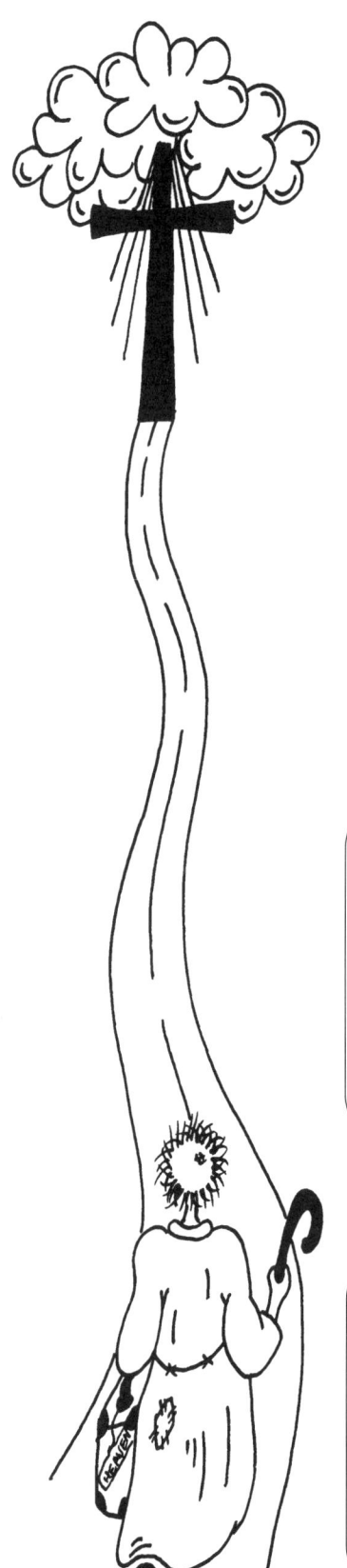

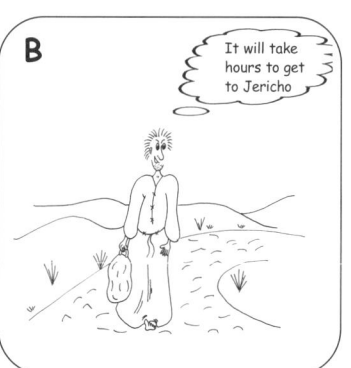

Do we care for other people?

It was clear that the Samaritan really did care for other people, even people who were regarded as enemies of his country. Can you think of any ways that we can show care for other people in this country and elsewhere?

_____

_____

_____

Draw two pictures:
A picture from Jesus' parable
A picture showing how we can help today

Extra challenge

Write down:
Ways that we should support people who have suffered from crimes, *or*
Ways to prevent crimes from happening.

Lesson 15
Putting faith into practice

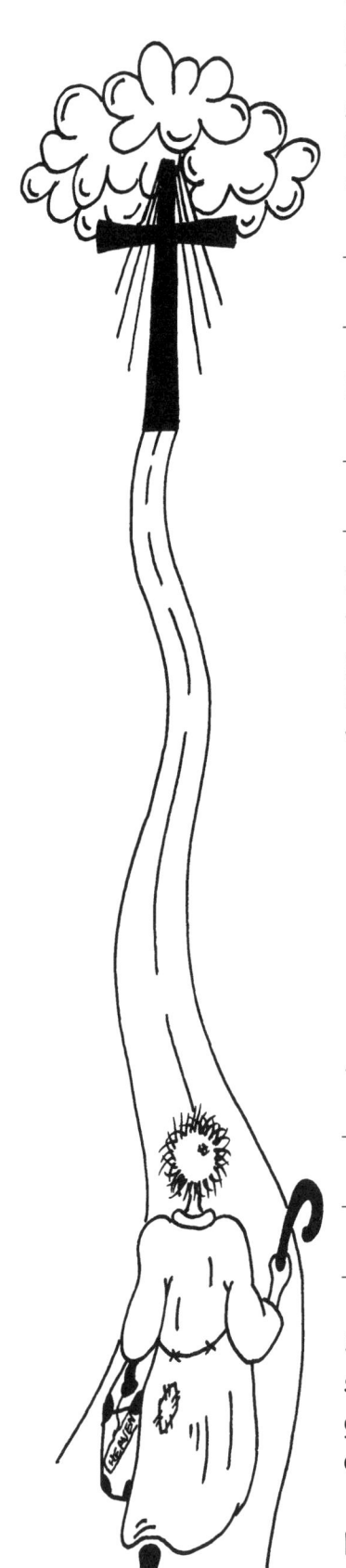

Imagine that you had made a mistake which caused you a lot of problems. You decided to ask a friend for advice, but when you told them what had happened, they turned to you and snarled: 'It serves you right! If you had used your common sense things would have been very different. Don't expect me to help you now!'
What would you think of that friend?

_____

_____

How do you think the friend *should* have acted?

_____

_____

If we want to be Christians we will want to live life's journey being faithful to our Lord Jesus Christ, and that will mean that every part of our life will be changed! This will particularly involve two important parts of our lives. To find out what these are, read the verses just before the parable of the Good Samaritan.

 Luke 10:25-38
Every Christian should love God with all their heart, soul, strength and mind and their neighbour as themselves.

Think of ways we can show God that we love him:

_____

_____

_____

Showing God's love to people does not mean romantic love! It is the self-giving love that Jesus showed when he went to the cross. He gave everything for us, and that means that we should want to do all we can for others.

There are several ways that we can show the love of God to people. We can do whatever we are able to in helping the people we meet day by day, but with the help of various organisations we can help people far beyond.

Some ways you can enjoy helping other people.

But remember to check at home first.

Through the local Church
The local Church gives some money to help local people in difficulties and also helps in practical ways.

Through medical charities
Money spent at their shops will help people to find out how to cure more diseases and relieve suffering.

Through missionary societies
They do all kinds of work to help other people as well as talking about Jesus. If you are interested they will send details of some of their work.

Through youth organisations
Groups like Church Lads' and Church Girls' Brigade, Boys' Brigade, Girls' Brigade, Scouts and Guides often help you to help others.

Through other groups
Other local groups do important work in helping others.

Colour this picture of people helping others

Extra challenge

Write about ways that you could help other people (both the people you meet each day and also people who have great needs).

Lesson 16: Faith in action – Saint Paul

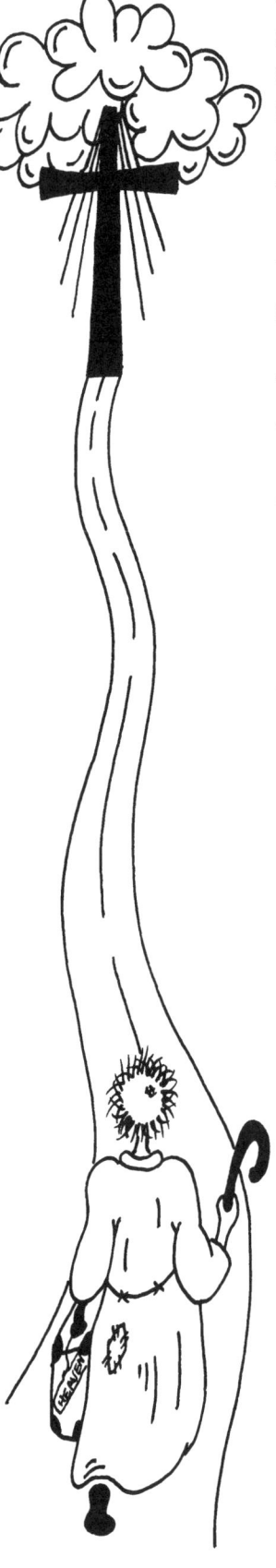

In this part of our lessons we are going to think about some great Christian people down the ages, and find out about their life's journey. Today we are considering Saint Paul. Paul was a faithful Jew who was born just a few years after Jesus. He wasn't brought up in Jerusalem, but in the Greek-speaking seaport of Tarsus. However, he was so keen to follow the law that he went to Jerusalem to learn from the great teacher, Gamaliel.

When Paul heard about Christians saying that God had spoken through Jesus he was furious, and tried to stop the Christian faith growing.

He was so keen to stop the Christians that he had a lot to do with the Christian, Saint Stephen, being put to death; he also led a team to Damascus so that he could bring Christians to Jerusalem in chains to face trial, but God had other ideas! *Read all about what happened to Paul.*

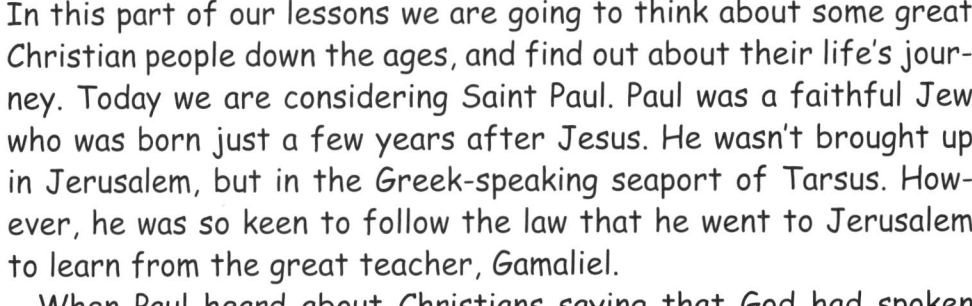

Read Acts 9:1-6, 17-21

From then onwards, Paul became what he called a 'new creation!' He realised that knowing Jesus made him like a new person, and he wanted to tell everyone about Jesus.

Paul was a brave man. Often he was in danger because of wanting to tell people about Jesus, but his life's journey with Jesus was so exciting that he didn't mind.

Today it is possible to board a plane and be on the other side of the world in a day and a half. Paul had to walk or travel by sailing boat or on the back of animals – yet he still managed to take the Good News about Jesus as far as Rome, about a thousand miles away!

This is what he wrote in 2 Corinthians 11:24-28, 12:10 as he approached the end of his life:

Five times I was given thirty-nine lashes by the Jews: three times I was whipped by the Romans; and once I was stoned. I have been in three shipwrecks, and once I spent twenty-four hours in the water. In my many travels I have been in danger of floods and from robbers, in danger from fellow Jews and from Gentiles; there have been dangers in cities, dangers in the wilds, dangers from high seas and dangers from false friends . . . I have been hungry and thirsty; I have often been without enough food, shelter or clothing . . .

I am content with weaknesses, insults, hardships, persecutions and difficulties for Christ's sake, for when I am weak, then I am strong.

(Paul meant that he was weak in body but strong in his faith.)

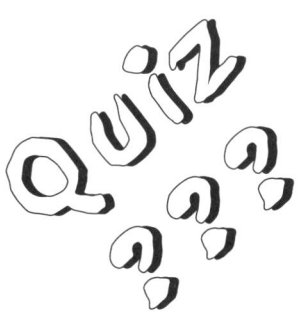

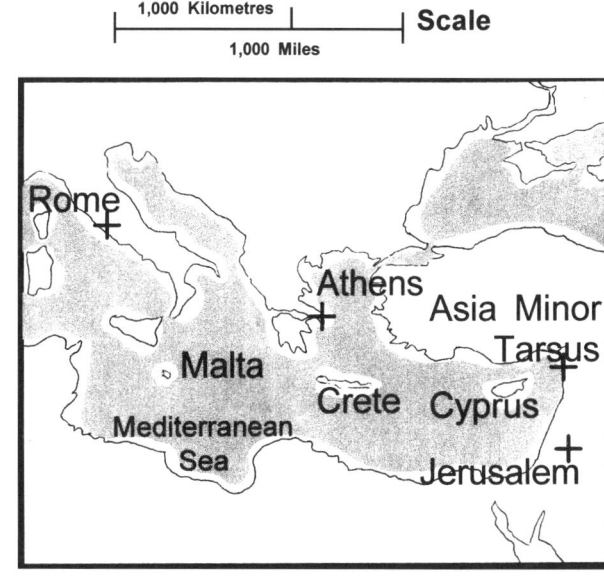

Some places Saint Paul visited

First find these words in the square and cross them out. (They may read forwards, backwards, up or down but not diagonally.)

Antioch   Myra
Arabia   Paphos
Berea   Perga
Cyprus   Rome
Derbe   Tarsus
Jerusalem   Tyre
Lystra

S	A	I	N	J	T	L	P	T
A	A	U	L	E	T	Y	O	Y
N	C	Y	P	R	U	S	B	R
T	A	R	S	U	S	T	E	E
I	O	K	T	S	H	R	R	B
O	A	I	B	A	R	A	E	R
C	G	E	G	L	O	R	A	E
H	R	S	P	E	E	Y	L	D
T	E	R	O	M	E	M	O	R
O	P	A	P	H	O	S	M	E

Then copy the remaining letters into the grid below to give a special message. Work left to right along each row in turn.

_ _ _ _ _   _ _ _ _   _ _ _ _   _ _ _
_ _ _ _ _ _   _ _   _ _ _ _.

Extra challenge

Find out and write about the kinds of dangers Paul and his friends might have met when travelling by ship. (Also see Acts 27:13-44.)

Lesson 17: Faith in action – Francis of Assisi

Down the centuries there have been very many ordinary people who lived as faithful Christians from day to day (as many still do). Some, however, make a huge impression on the world around them, and these are the people we are considering just now. The star of today's lesson lived about 800 years ago, and his name is Francis of Assisi.

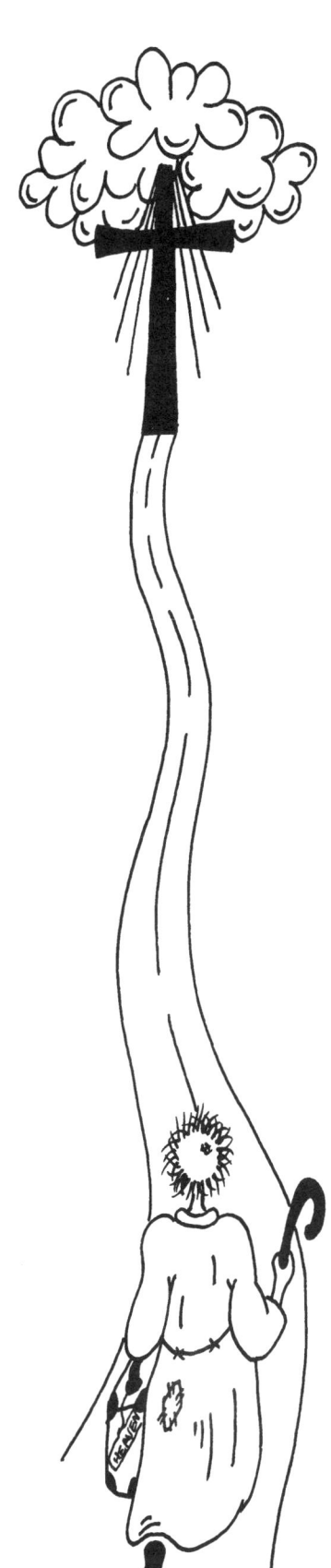

People often think of Saint Francis as the friend of animals – and it is true that he was a gentle person who was kind to animals – but he did so much more than that.

His father was rich and he started to live a worldly life. He spent some time as a prisoner of war, when he decided to change his way of life. He started to help people suffering from leprosy and restored broken-down church buildings. His father was furious and turned against him.

Then, in the year 1208 when Francis was 26 years old, his life's journey took another big turn. One day while he was praying he realised that the words of Matthew 10:5-12 were very special to him, and that God was calling him to his main work.

Francis found a team of twelve people who became known as Franciscans; they joined him in his preaching and soon a woman called Clare started a similar team of women, called the Order of the Poor Ladies.

Read Matthew 10:7-13

When he tried to reach the Holy Land he was prevented by a shipwreck, but he did preach in Egypt, Spain, Morocco and his own homeland of Italy.

He died at just 44 years of age in the year 1226, but the work he did is still an inspiration to countless people even today.

Crossword

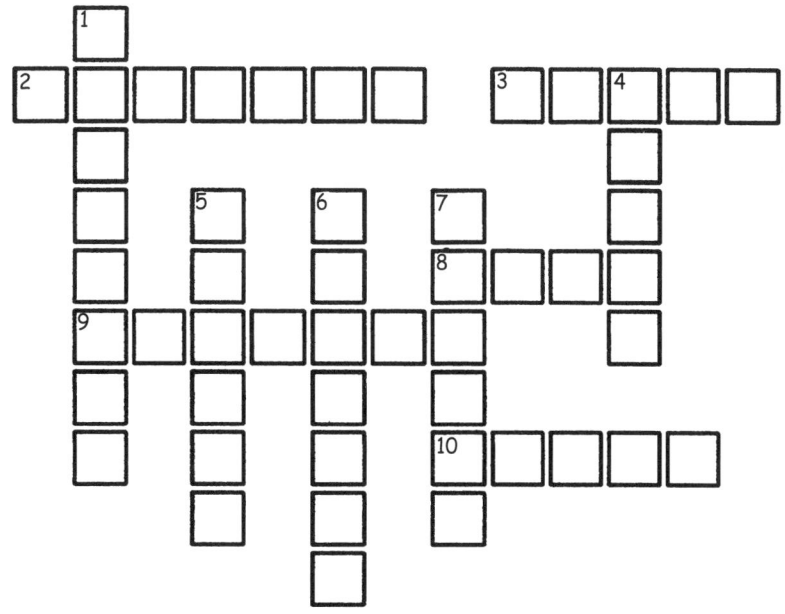

Clues

1. Middle Eastern land that Francis tried to reach.
2. A country in north-west Africa he went to.
3. See clue 8.
4. A country in north-east Africa he went to.
5. Where he was sent when captured in battle.
6. Name of the man who founded the Franciscans!
7. The town where answer 6 lived.
8./3. It happened when answer 6 tried to reach answer 1.
9. As well as people, Francis also liked these.
10. A south-west European country he visited.

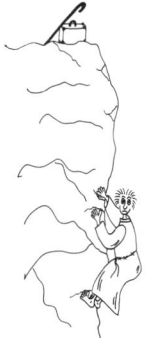

Extra challenge

Do six drawings of the work of Saint Francis, in order.
At different stages in his life different things were important to him.
What is important to you today?

Lesson 18: Faith in action – John Wesley

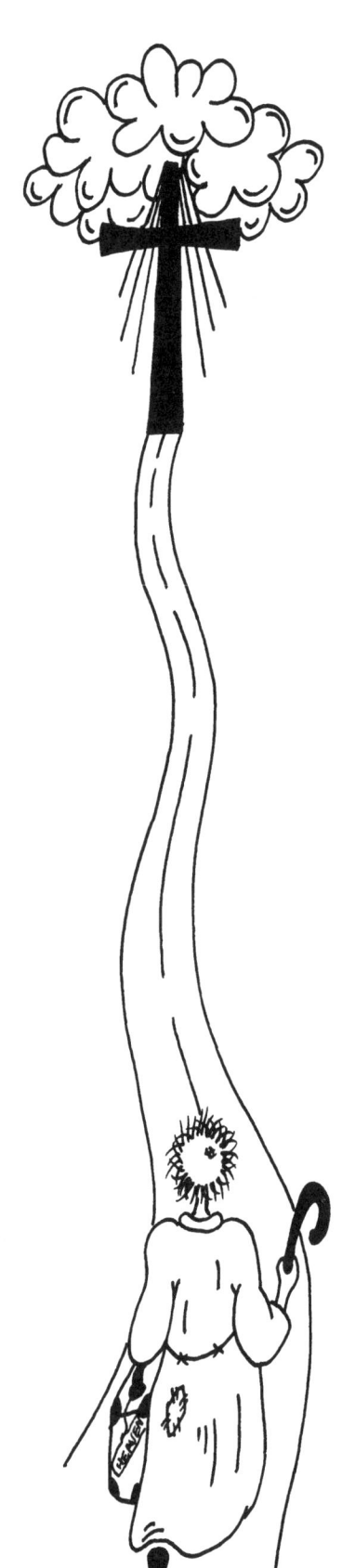

We have recently thought about two of the best-known Christians ever – Saint Paul who lived almost two thousand years ago, and Saint Francis, who lived about eight hundred years ago. The man we are considering this week was born about 300 years ago, in 1703 and died in 1791.

John Wesley was the 11th son of an Anglican vicar. He became a clergyman himself and was his father's assistant curate. Later he went to Oxford University, and he and friends joined the Holy Club and went to visit prisoners and comfort sick people. Despite all this he was not satisfied with his life. His life's journey was not going in the right direction! Some people laughed at their methodical approach and called them 'Methodists'. They later adopted that name for themselves!

He decided to travel to America to be a missionary, but he still didn't appreciate the peace that God wanted him to have. His work was a failure and he returned in 1738. Later that year he went to a service in the Moravian Chapel in London. When he heard God's word read he said that his heart was 'strangely warmed' and he began to appreciate that he had desperately needed faith in Jesus Christ alone – there was no substitute for that!

The Church of England had a lot of failings at the time. It had no idea how to reach many of the people in this country. Wesley now had such a living faith that he wasn't happy just to preach in Church buildings! He started travelling about 5,000 miles each year round England on horseback telling people about Jesus.

Read Romans 3:21-24 This tells us about the kind of life that Wesley started to live.

John Wesley preached about the good news as long as he lived, and after he died many of the people he had helped started the Methodist Church, which has millions of members worldwide.

First find these words in the square and cross them out. (They may read forwards, backwards, up or down, but not diagonally.)

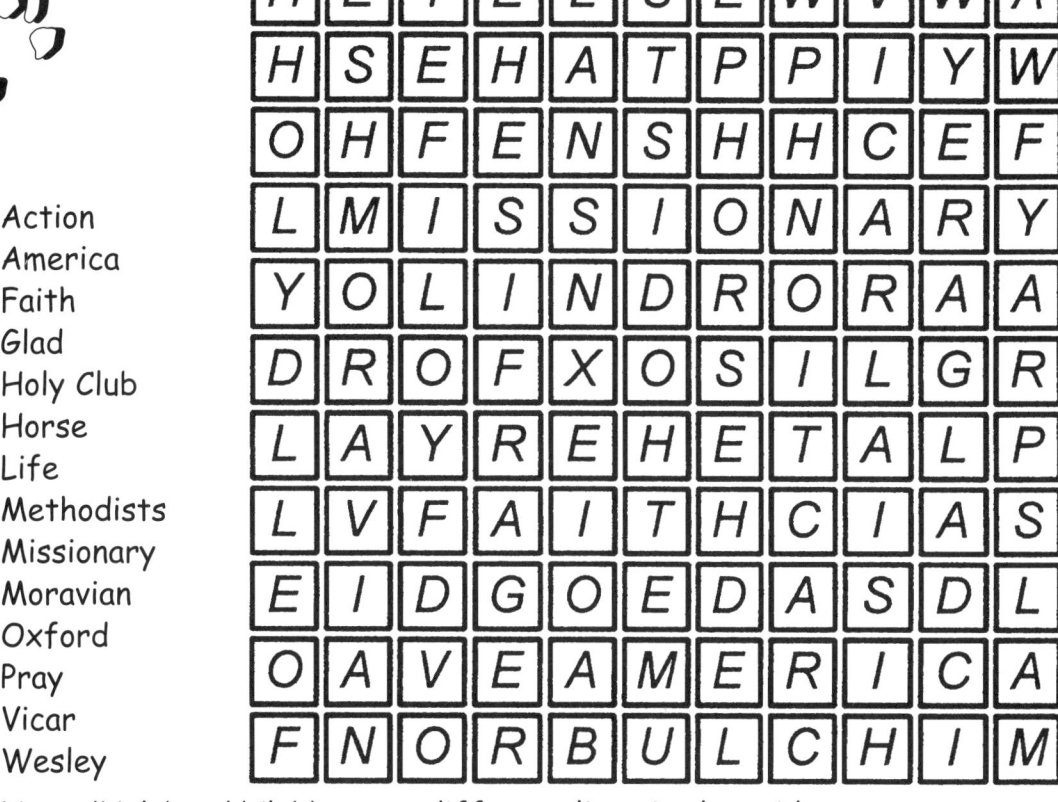

Action
America
Faith
Glad
Holy Club
Horse
Life
Methodists
Missionary
Moravian
Oxford
Pray
Vicar
Wesley

Note: 'Holy' and 'Club' are on different lines in the grid.

Then copy the remaining letters into the grid below to give a special message. Work from left to right along each row in turn.

__ ___ _____ ____ __ _____

_____ ____ ____ ___ ___.

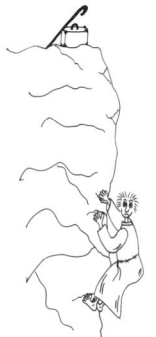

Extra challenge

In some ways the world today is as it was when John Wesley was at work, but in other ways it is very different. Write about the good and the bad changes since then. What do you think the Church should do to make its message heard and understood today?

Lesson 19: Faith in action – Mother Teresa

The last person we are considering in this series on faith in action achieved amazing things in the twentieth century, despite the fact that she was a tiny person, and that she was born in a country where it was illegal to be a Christian! Mother Teresa was born in Albania in 1910 and was originally called Agnes Gonxha Bojaxhiu. Her parents moved to Yugoslavia later, and by the age of 18 she was in Ireland where she joined a convent of the Sisters of our Lady of Loretto.

She trained as a teacher and became the principal of a high school in Calcutta in India. While she was there she was horrified by the sight of so many sick and dying people on the streets. She knew that this was very wrong, and she was determined to do something about it, although she didn't really know what at first. Eventually she left teaching to work with homeless people.

Read Matthew 25:31-40

Mother Teresa took the above reading to heart and said that she thought the sick and poor were the 'embodiment of Christ'.

She was saddened that many people were so poor that they lived and died on the streets, so she opened the Pure Heart Home for Dying Destitutes in 1952. She wanted poor people to be able to be cared for when they needed it most.

She was determined to do all she could to ease the difficulties that poor people had to face, and that meant that she was not frightened of challenging the rich in India and elsewhere, and she was eventually one of the few foreign people in India who could challenge the governing classes about wrong laws and policies.

Although she worked in India from the 1930s until her death in 1997, her faith, courage and self-giving became known in all the world, and in 1979 she was given the Nobel Peace Prize in recognition of her tremendous work. She also inspired similar work in many other cities in this country and around the world.

God does not ask every Christian to live in poverty, but he does ask us to be prepared to do so if that is right for us.

In this quiz you must find the missing words by looking at your Bible. The clue number is written after the word like this: *1. Then transfer the words to the correct boxes, and follow the arrow to find the words reading downwards.

*1
*2
*3
*4
*5
*6
*7
*8
*9
*10
*11
*12

(v 31) When the Son of _ _ _ *1 comes as King and all the angels with him, he will sit on his _ _ _ _ _ *2 throne, (v 32) and the people of all the _ _ _ _ _ _ _ _ *3 will be gathered before him. Then he will divide them into two groups, just as a shepherd seperates the _ _ _ _ _ *4 from the goats. (v 33) Then he will put the _ _ _ _ _ _ _ _ _ *5 people on his _ _ _ _ _ _ *6 hand and others on his left. (v 34) Then the King will say to the people on his right, 'Come, you that are blessed by my _ _ _ _ _ _ ! *7 Come and _ _ _ _ _ _ _ _ *8 the Kingdom which has been prepared for you ever since the creation of the world. (v 35) I was hungry and you fed me, _ _ _ _ _ _ _ _ *9 and you gave me a drink, I was a stranger and you received me in your homes, (v 36) naked and you clothed me, I was sick and you took care of me, in prison and you _ _ _ _ _ _ _ _ *10 me.' (v 37) The righteous will then answer him. 'When, Lord, did we ever see you hungry and feed you, or thirsty and give you a drink? (v 38) When did we ever see you a stranger and welcome you in our homes, or naked and clothe you? (v 39) When did we ever see you _ _ _ _ *11 or in prison and visit you?' (v 40) The King will reply, 'I tell you, whenever you did this for one of the least important of these members of my _ _ _ _ _ _ , *12 you did it for me!'

What are the words that you are looking for?

_ _ _ _ _ _ _ _ _ _ _ _

Extra challenge

Write about 'A day in the life of Mother Teresa'. Is there anybody that you can help today?

Lesson 20
Rules and guidelines - the Ten Commandments

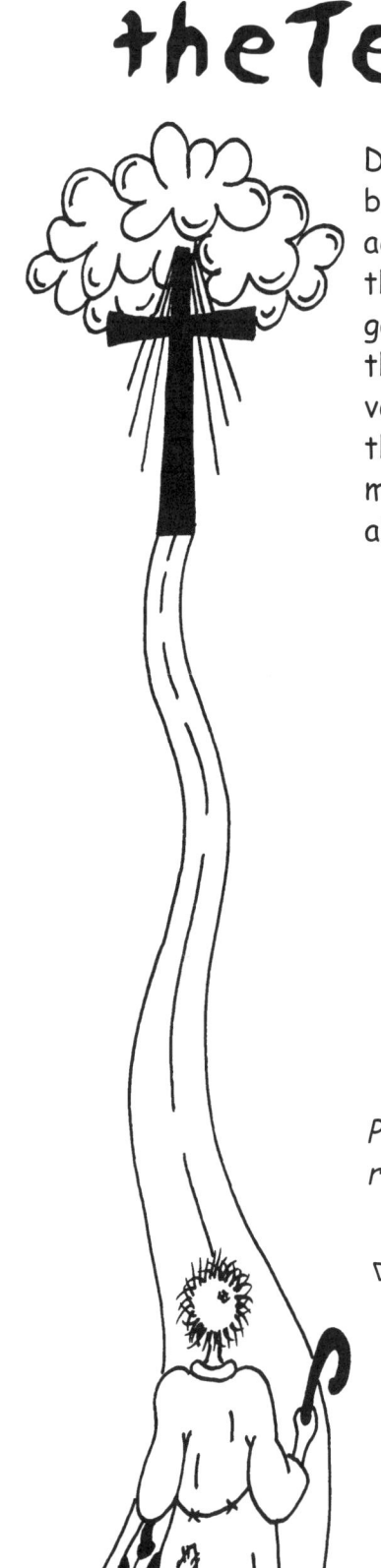

Do you remember Moses? He was the one who obeyed God and brought the children of Israel away from slavery in Egypt and across the Red Sea towards the land which God promised. When they reached that land they would need rules to live by, and so God gave Moses the Ten Commandments. These Commandments were the law for the people of Israel, but they also form the basis of very many other laws, and give people the best idea how to live their lives. Christians and Jewish believers take these Commandments as vital to their lives. It is worth trying to remember them all! They are so very important.

The Ten Commandments

1. I am the Lord your God, worship no god but me.
2. Do not make or worship any idol.
3. Do not use my name for evil purposes.
4. Observe the Sabbath and keep it holy.
5. Respect your father and your mother.
6. Do not commit murder.
7. Do not commit adultery.
8. Do not steal.
9. Do not accuse anyone falsely.
10. Do not desire what another person owns.

Put a number by each statement to show which Commandment it refers to

Don't be greedy.

Be honest in all you say about people.

If we worship any idol (or anybody or anything else) we cannot be really dedicated to God.

God is great, and cares for us. We should never use his name wrongly.

God made us, and wants us to appreciate him, and give him the honour that he deserves.

People who despise the guidance of parents usually become bad adults.

We must realise and appreciate the value of every other person, even the ones we don't like.

God who made us knows how we work best. We need time for prayer and rest.

Realise the value of marriage and family life. No one should ever do anything that can damage it.

It belongs to someone else, so I will not take it from her or him.

Quiz ???

See if you can discover how these people break any of the Ten Commandments, and which ones they are breaking.

In each of the groups of letters, write the one that is repeated downwards, and the answers will spell out a message.

```
J E Q P      P Y E      C A M A H N D M E N T S
K E W A      O E V      O S O M A O O O V O R O
A A E P      I S E      M C M B Y Z J E N A M
B I R E      U H N      I H E N E H Y D R E N E
K O T R      Y A T      C O N C S I D C H M T S
Y U Y I      T H I      A O T M A N I B I U L U
Z K E Q      T O O      L L S D I G G M M R E N

- - - -      - - -      - - - - - - - - - - - -

A S R      P P B A G      W I T H      A G T
F P E      U E A C I      O N R O      L L L
F O F      R R L C B      T I U P      P I U
O O R      P F A E E      I B T I      H M M
R L A      L E N P R      W A H U      A U I
D E C      I C C T E      U L I T      B L L
S R T      T T E S T      L T E H      T T G

- - -      - - - - -      - - - -      - - -
```

Extra challenge

Write about some situations where it is difficult or impossible to keep all of the Ten Commandments. What should you do in those circumstances?

Lesson 21
Rules and guidelines –
Jesus sums up the law

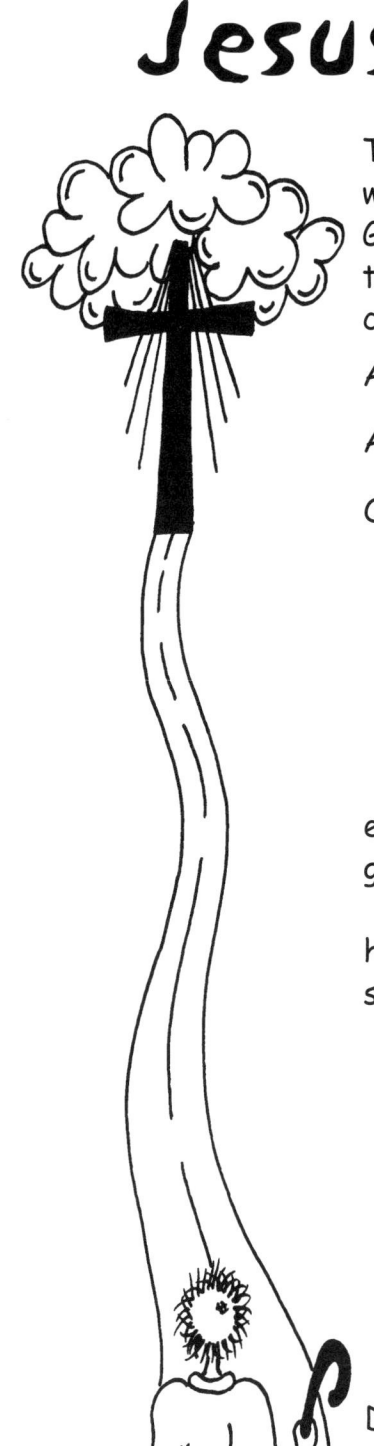

The Ten Commandments were, and still are, very important to anyone who wants to know more about how people are to live in peace with God and with each other. Look at the last sheet and see if you can tell which Commandments concern our thoughts and actions concerning God, and which are about our behaviour to each other.

About God _____

About people _____

One day Jesus was asked a question about the Commandments.
Read Mark 12:28-31

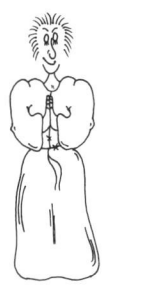

Jesus was explaining why the Commandments were the way they are. One of the problems was that people had had the Commandments for centuries – but they had been using them wrongly! They thought that God would be pleased if they kept every part of the law – and the extra rules that they had added themselves. They may have done good things but they were proud and critical.

When Jesus summed up the law he was not saying anything new; he was stating what had been written much earlier but many people seemed to have forgotten.

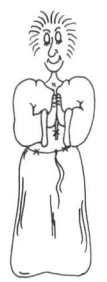 

Do the puzzle overleaf and then try the extra challenge.

Extra challenge

Write about ways that you could be more faithful to God and get on better with other people.

Shade in black the sections containing a small circle to see what the message is. If there is time, colour the whole page.

____ ___ ____ ____ ___ ____ ___ ____

_____, ____, ____ ___ _____ ___ ____

____ _____ __ _____.

Lesson 22
Rules and guidelines ~ The Beatitudes

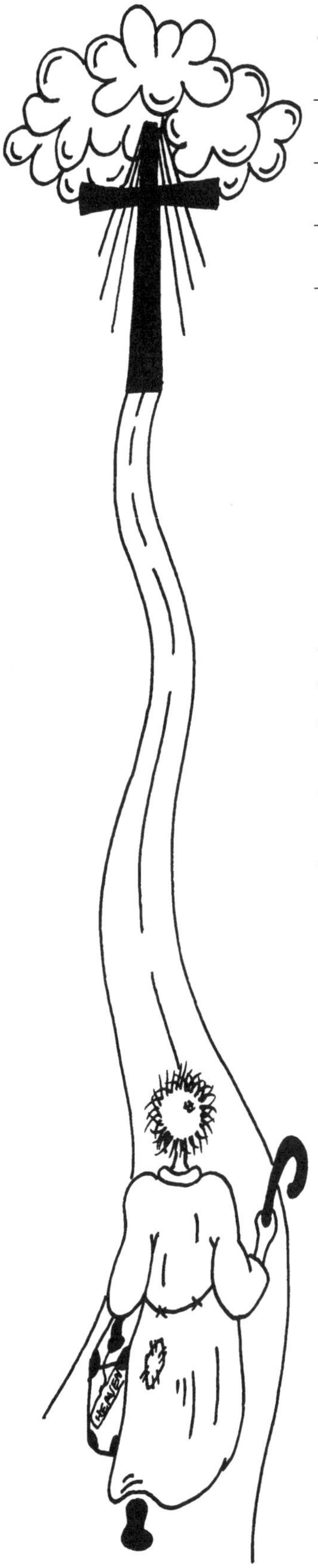

What are the kinds of things that make you happy?

_____
_____
_____
_____

Many people think that the best way to cope with life's journey is to be selfish and only look after yourself, but you can't do that and still be a friend of Jesus. In the Gospel of Matthew we can read about the 'Sermon on the Mount', when Jesus said many things about how life should be lived to the huge crowds who wanted to hear Him speak. He didn't give commands, but guidelines that we would be foolish to ignore. The first part of the sermon on the mount was the 'Beatitudes', which are about people who will be 'blessed' (or 'happy').

Read Matthew 5:3-12

Jesus was showing us that there is something much more important than selfishness. Faith is important – and if we have real faith it will result in us being the kind of people who have real joy at all times, because we will become closer to God and so we will want to follow Jesus' guidelines.

Quiz — TWIN TWIN

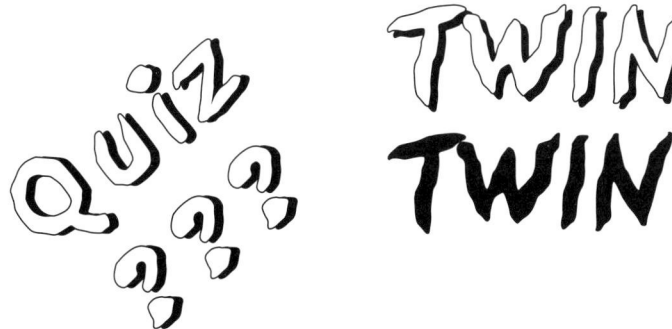

Twin the happy people with the reason for their happiness.

Jesus said, 'Happy are those who . . .

- A . . . know they are spiritually poor . . .
- B . . . mourn . . .
- C . . . are humble . . .
- D . . . want to do what God requires . . .
- E . . . are merciful . . .
- F . . . are pure in heart . . .
- G . . . work for peace . . .
- H . . . are persecuted because they do what God requires . . .
- I . . . are persecuted because they are my followers . . .

. . . because . . .

1 . . . God will call them his children.
2 . . . the Kingdom of heaven belongs to them.
3 . . . the Kingdom of heaven belongs to them.
4 . . . they will receive what God has promised.
5 . . . God will be merciful to them.
6 . . . a great reward is kept for them in heaven.
7 . . . God will comfort them.
8 . . . they will see God.
9 . . . God will satisfy them fully.

Put your answers here

A =
B =
C =
D =
E =
F =
G =
H =
I =

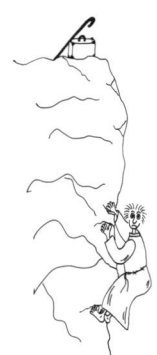

Extra challenge

Draw pictures, with speech bubbles, showing a peacemaker at work in the playground.

Lesson 23
Rules and guidelines ~ the fruit of the Spirit

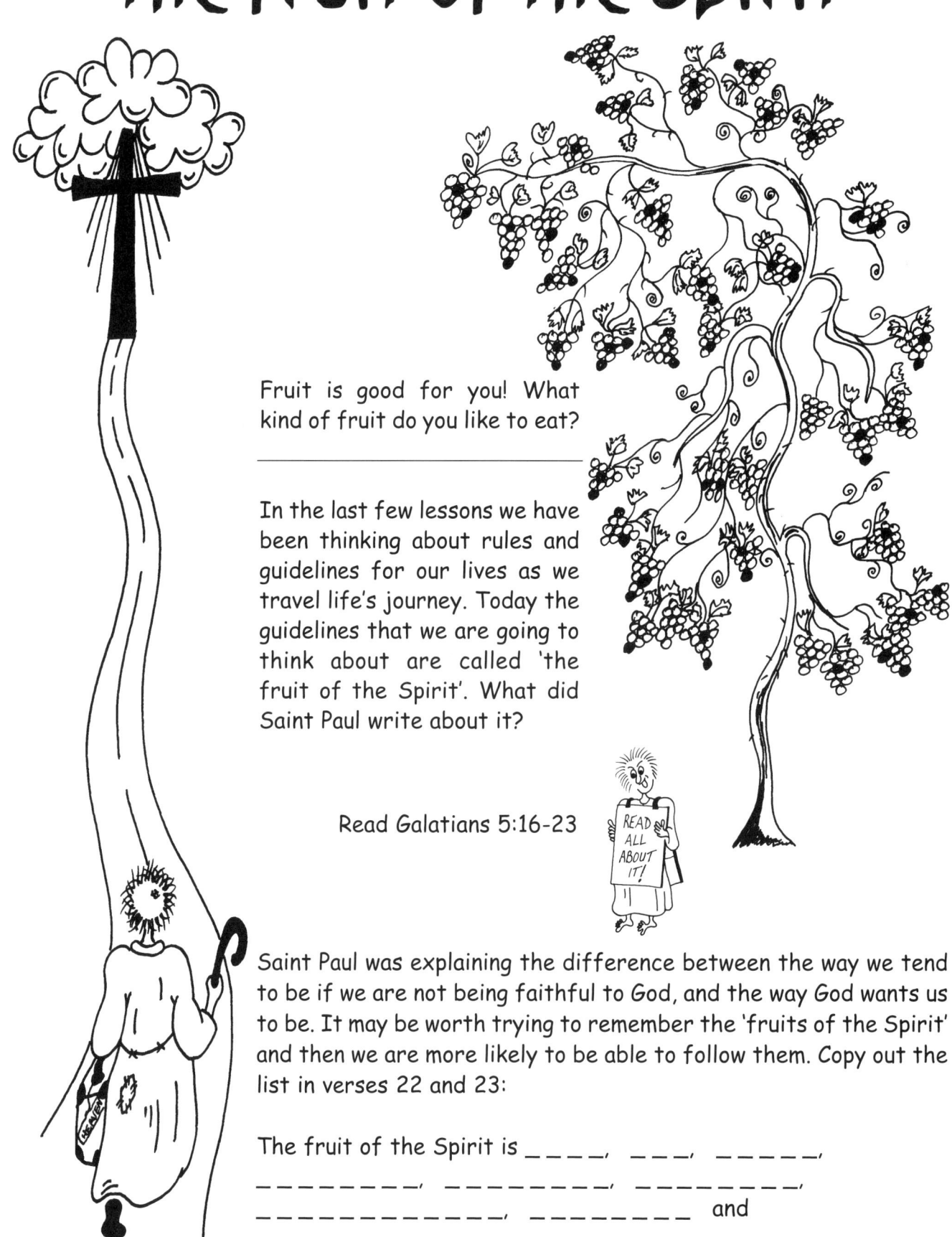

Fruit is good for you! What kind of fruit do you like to eat?

_____

In the last few lessons we have been thinking about rules and guidelines for our lives as we travel life's journey. Today the guidelines that we are going to think about are called 'the fruit of the Spirit'. What did Saint Paul write about it?

Read Galatians 5:16-23

Saint Paul was explaining the difference between the way we tend to be if we are not being faithful to God, and the way God wants us to be. It may be worth trying to remember the 'fruits of the Spirit' and then we are more likely to be able to follow them. Copy out the list in verses 22 and 23:

The fruit of the Spirit is _ _ _ _, _ _ _, _ _ _ _ _ _, _ _ _ _ _ _ _ _, _ _ _ _ _ _ _ _, _ _ _ _ _ _ _ _, _ _ _ _ _ _ _ _ _ _ _ _, _ _ _ _ _ _ _ _ _ and _ _ _ _ _ _ _ _ _ _ _.

L	U	A	P	T	N	I	A	S
C	A	P	N	S	T	K	H	S
E	F	A	R	E	U	I	I	E
S	T	T	O	L	F	N	T	N
S	H	I	E	F	S	D	P	L
E	P	E	A	C	E	N	I	U
N	R	N	L	O	V	E	I	F
D	T	C	B	N	E	S	S	H
O	E	E	E	T	N	S	I	T
O	N	Y	O	R	U	R	L	I
G	I	F	J	O	Y	E	?	A
H	U	M	I	L	I	T	Y	F

First find the names of the fruit of the Spirit in the square and cross them out. (They may be read forwards, backwards, up or down but not diagonally.) Then cross out the name 'Saint Paul'.

Then copy the remaining letters into the grid to give a special message. Work from left to right along each row in turn.

___ ___ _____ __ ___ _____
__ ____ __ ____ ____?

Extra challenge

Think of the way a person would act if the Fruit of the Spirit is showing in his or her life. Write and draw pictures to illustrate that person.

Answers

Lesson 1

All-powerful   Genesis 1:1-3; Job 38:1-11
In all places   I Kings 8:27; Psalm 139:7-8
All-knowing   Psalm 139:1-6, 17-18
All-loving   Matthew 24:37; Revelation 1:4-6

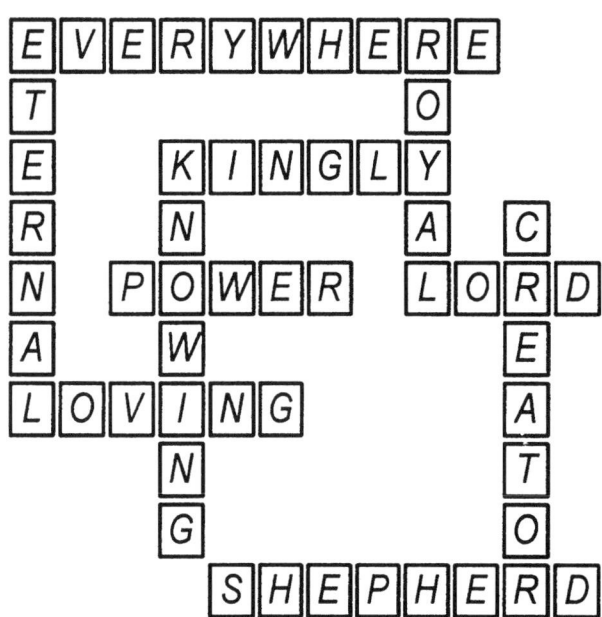

Lesson 2

Christians should approach Advent thoughtfully and with prayer.

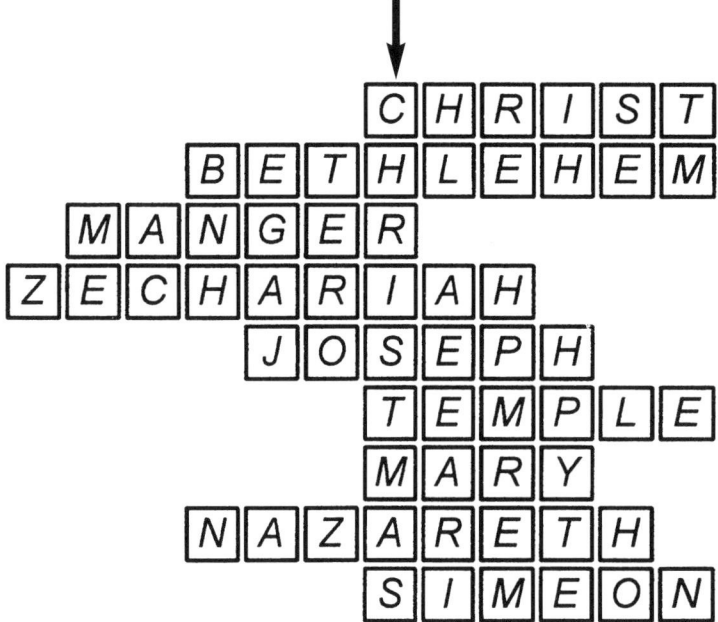

The word you are looking for is Christmas.

Order of drawings:

2	5	3
6	1	4

Lesson 3

(Initials in bold type)

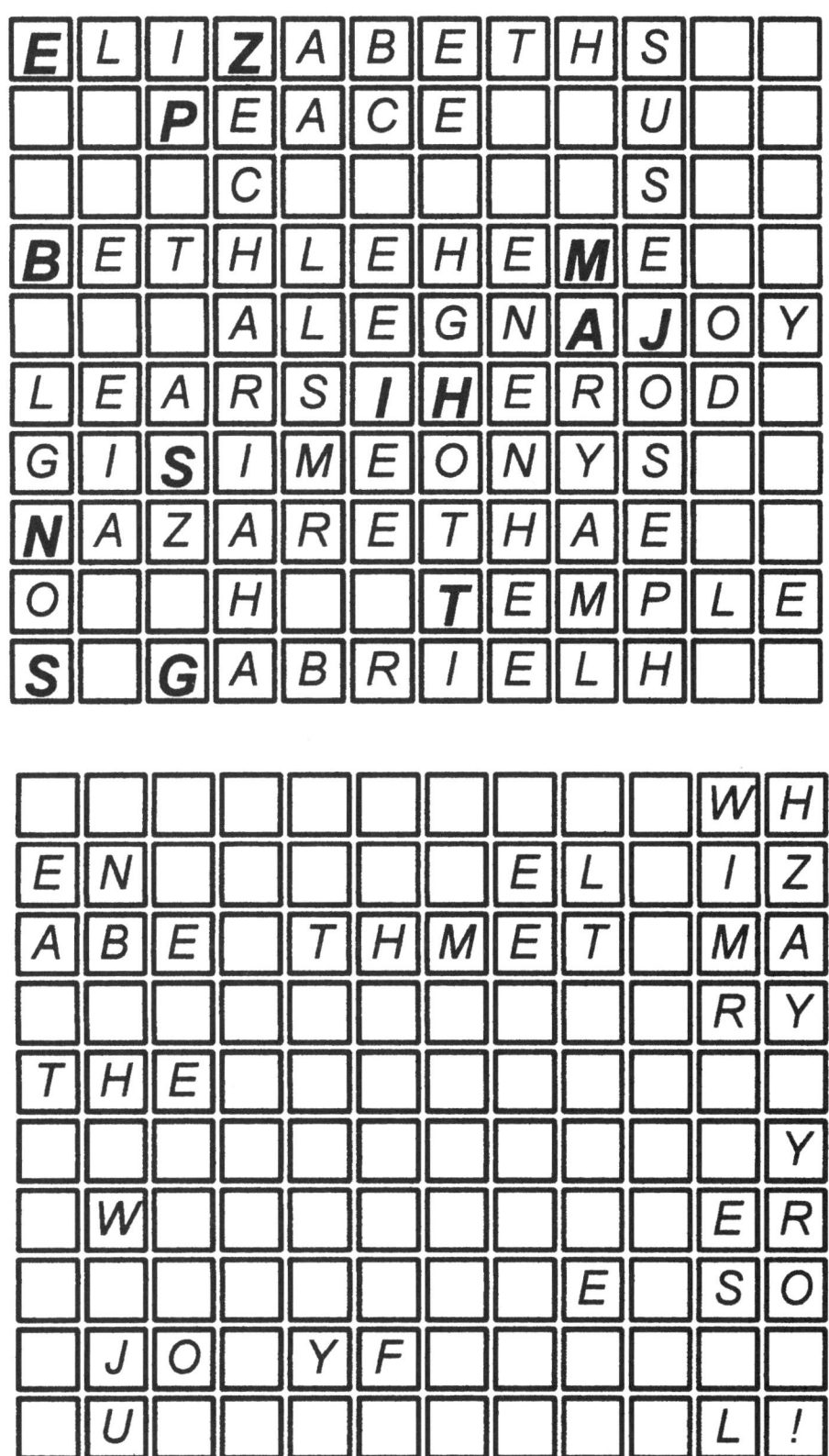

When Elizabeth met Mary they were so joyful!

LIFE'S JOURNEY

Lesson 4

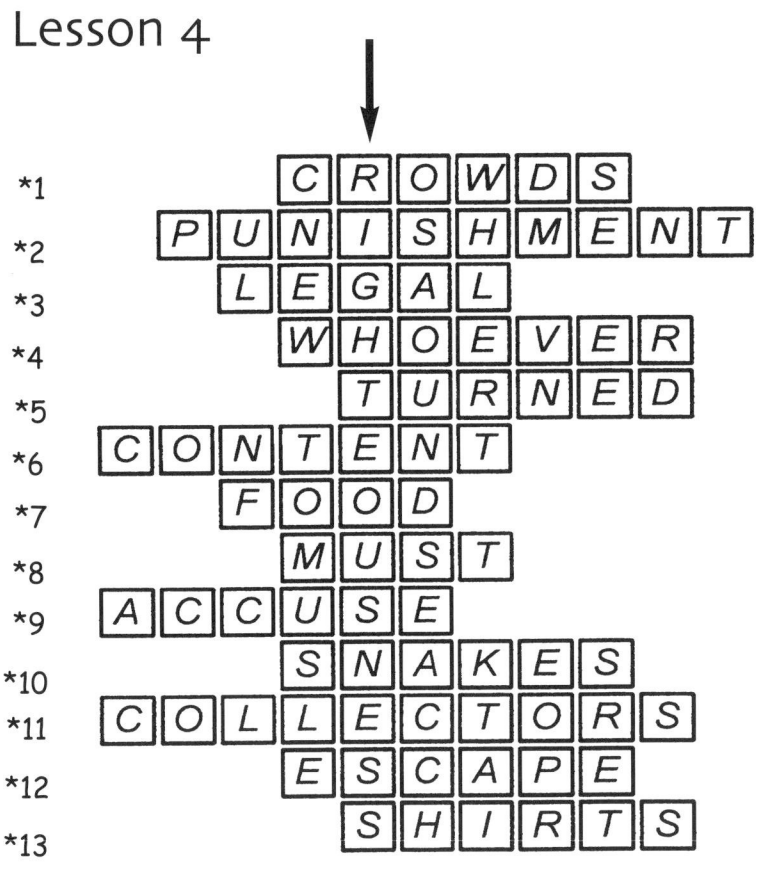

*1
*2
*3
*4
*5
*6
*7
*8
*9
*10
*11
*12
*13

(v 7) *Crowds* of people came out to John to be baptised by him. 'You *snakes*!', he said to them. 'Who told you that you could *escape* from the *punishment* God is about to send? (v 8) Do those things that will show that you have *turned* from your sins . . .'

(v 10) The people asked him, 'What are we to do then?' (v 11) He answered, 'Whoever has two *shirts* must give to the one who has none, and *whoever* has food *must* share it.'

(v 12) Some tax *collectors* came to be baptised, and they asked him, 'Teacher, what are we to do?' (v 13) 'Don't collect more than what is *legal*,' he told them.

(v 14) Some soldiers also asked him, 'What about us? What are we to do?' He said to them, 'Don't take money from anyone by force or *accuse* anyone *falsely*. Be content with your pay.'

Lesson 5

The leader was *Moses* and his brother was Aaron.

1. Today will be New Year's Day for you.
2. On the tenth day of the month choose a lamb or young goat.
3. In two weeks' time kill the animals.
4. Put some of the animal's blood around the doorpost so that your sons will be spared.
5. Get dressed ready for a journey, you will be leaving soon.
6. Roast the meat and have a good feed, but eat it quickly.
7. Do not leave any food, anything uneaten must be burnt.
8. Do not leave the house until morning, then leave this land quickly.

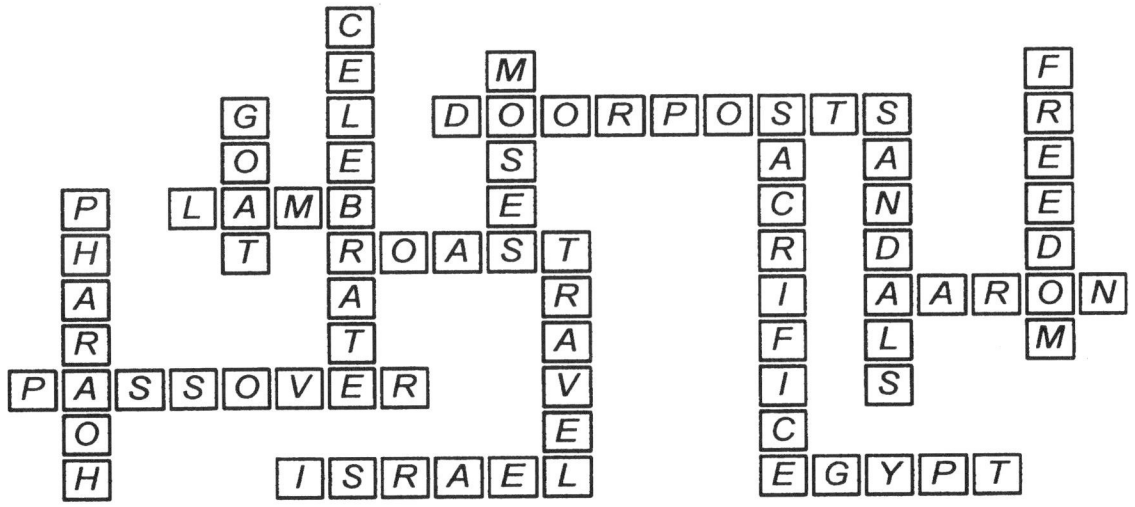

72

ANSWERS

Lesson 6

(Initial letters in bold type)

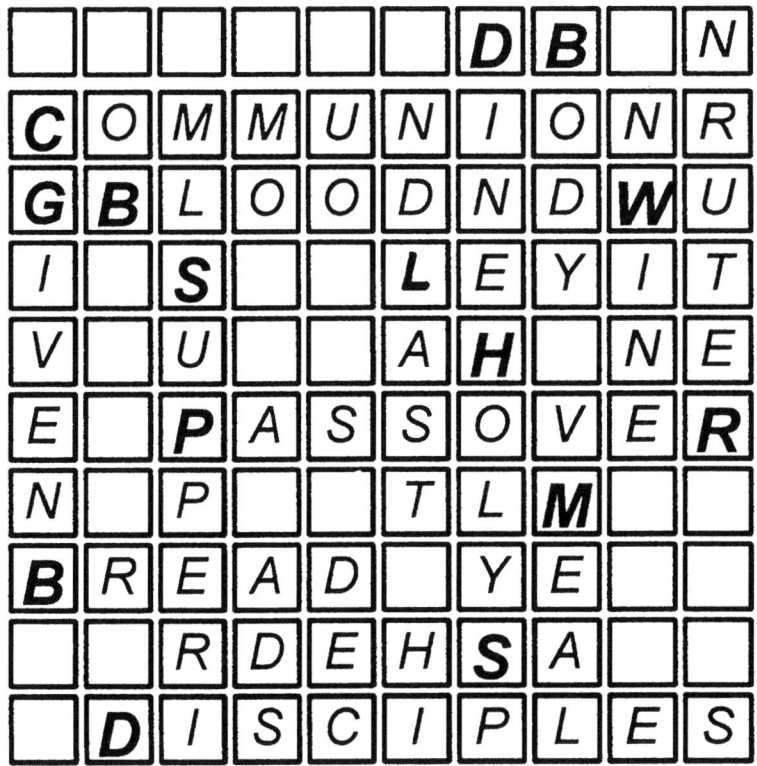

Lesson 7

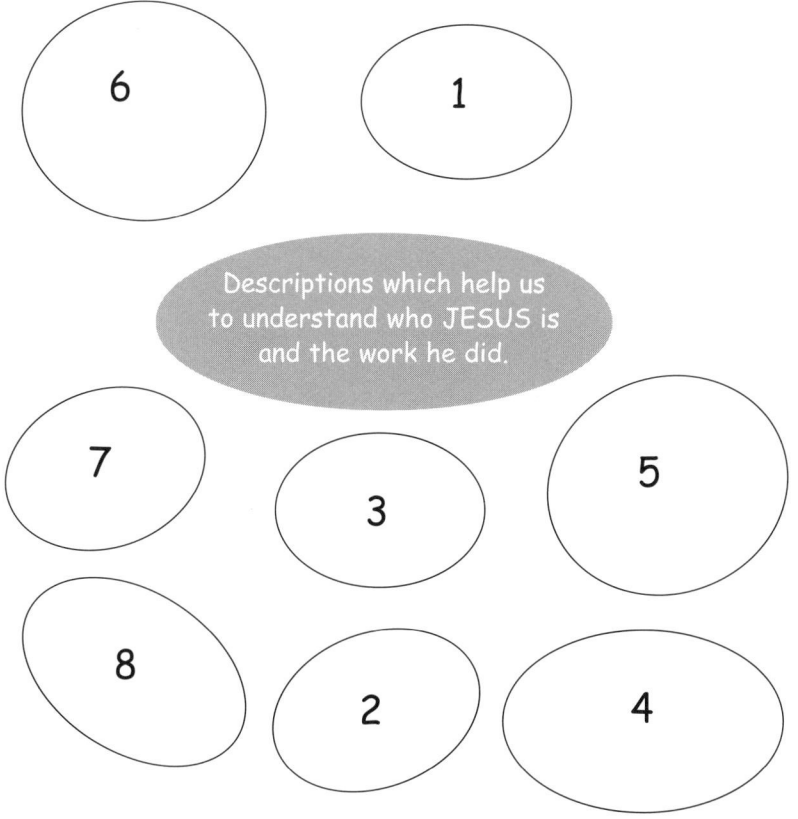

Descriptions which help us to understand who JESUS is and the work he did.

1. Light of the World
2. Son
3. Bread of Life
4. Save his people from their sins
5. Teacher
6. Lamb of God
7. Gate
8. Vine

LIFE'S JOURNEY

Lesson 8

1. Jesus told his disciples to untie something. What was it?
   A donkey.

2. How often had it been ridden?
   It had never been ridden.

3. When they untied the donkey, somebody complained, but they said what Jesus had told them to say. What was it?
   The Lord needs it.

4. What was used as a saddle?
   Coats.

5. A crowd of people appeared. What kind of people?
   Disciples, enthusiastic, noisy.

6. What did they throw on the road?
   Cloaks (and palm branches).

7. What did they shout?
   God bless the King who comes in the name of the Lord!
   Peace in heaven and glory to God.
   (Hosanna! – which means 'save us')

Note: The answers in brackets are from the other Gospels and are not mentioned in Luke.

Lesson 9

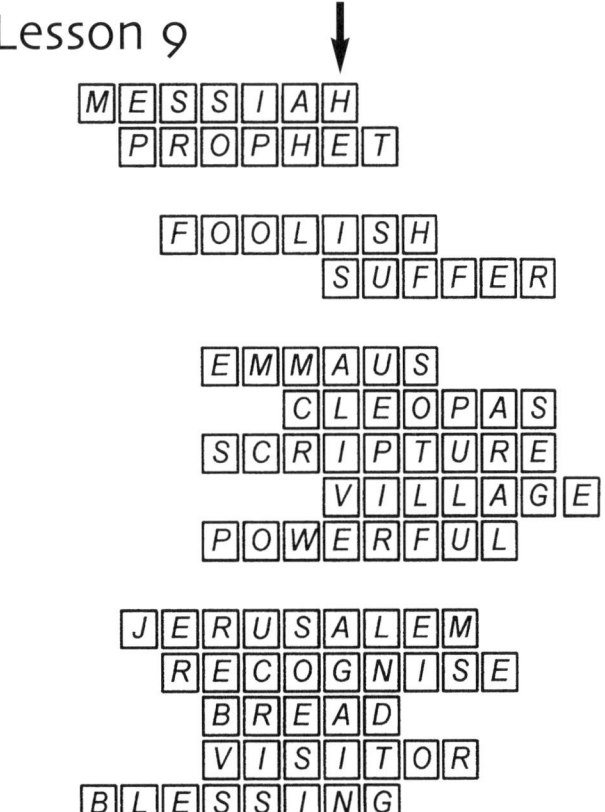

ANSWERS

Lesson 10

What had to happen before Jesus died? (v 46)
He suffered.

What happened next?
He rose from death three days later.

What would the disciples (and future Christians) have to do? (v 47)
In Jesus' name preach the message about salvation and forgiveness of sins to all nations, beginning from Jerusalem.

The disciples didn't see Jesus after that. Where did he go? (v 51)
To heaven.

The sentence is: He went up to heaven & sent them out into the world.

Lesson 11

A noise from the sky like a strong wind. (v 2)

They saw tongues of fire which spread out and touched each person there. (v 3)

They were filled with the Holy Spirit and began to speak in other languages as the Spirit enabled them to speak.

The Holy Spirit was given so that the followers of Jesus were able to stop being frightened of admitting that they were Christians, and they started to tell people about him, so soon there were many who joined them.

Lesson 13

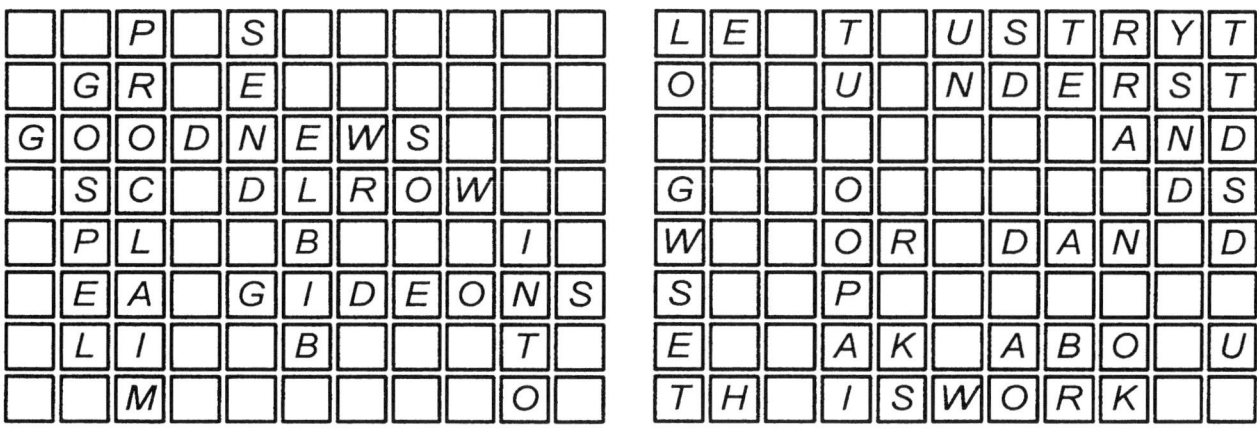

The sentence reads: Let us try to understand God's Word and speak about his work.

(See pages 9-11 to find out about Bible books.)

Lesson 14

A = 2
B = 1
C = 4
D = 5
E = 3
F = 6

Lesson 16

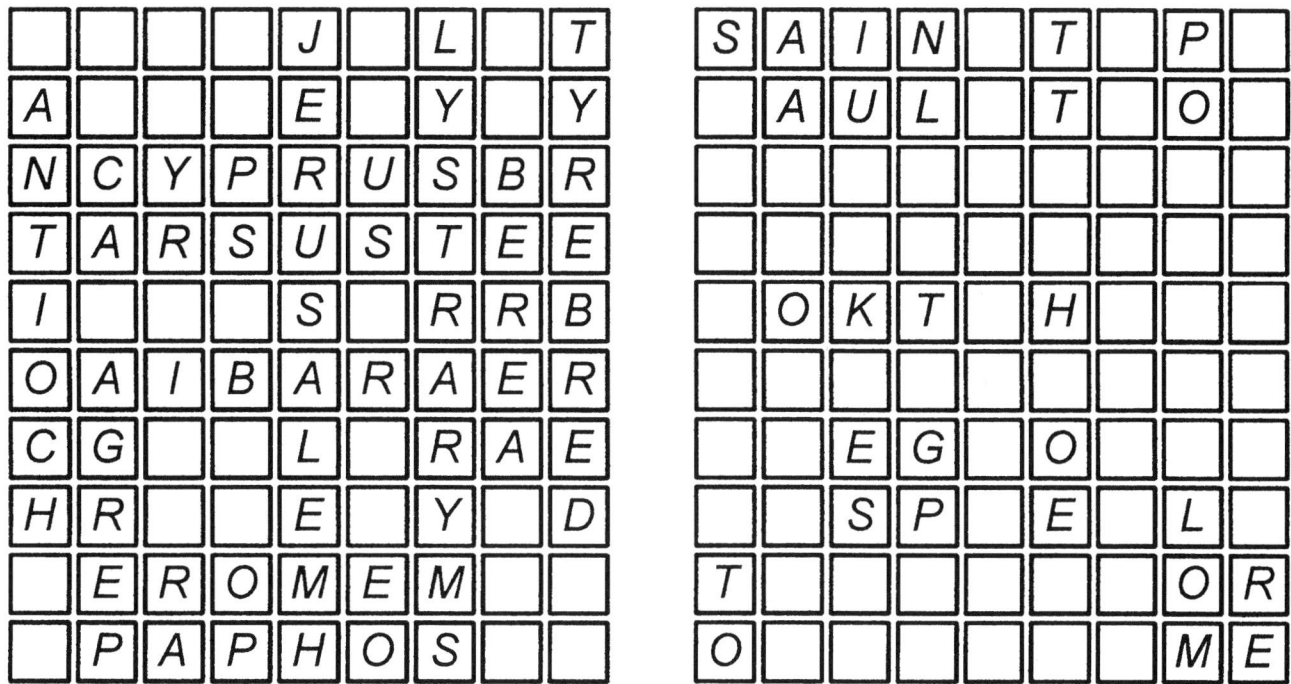

The letters spell: Saint Paul took the Gospel to Rome.

Lesson 17

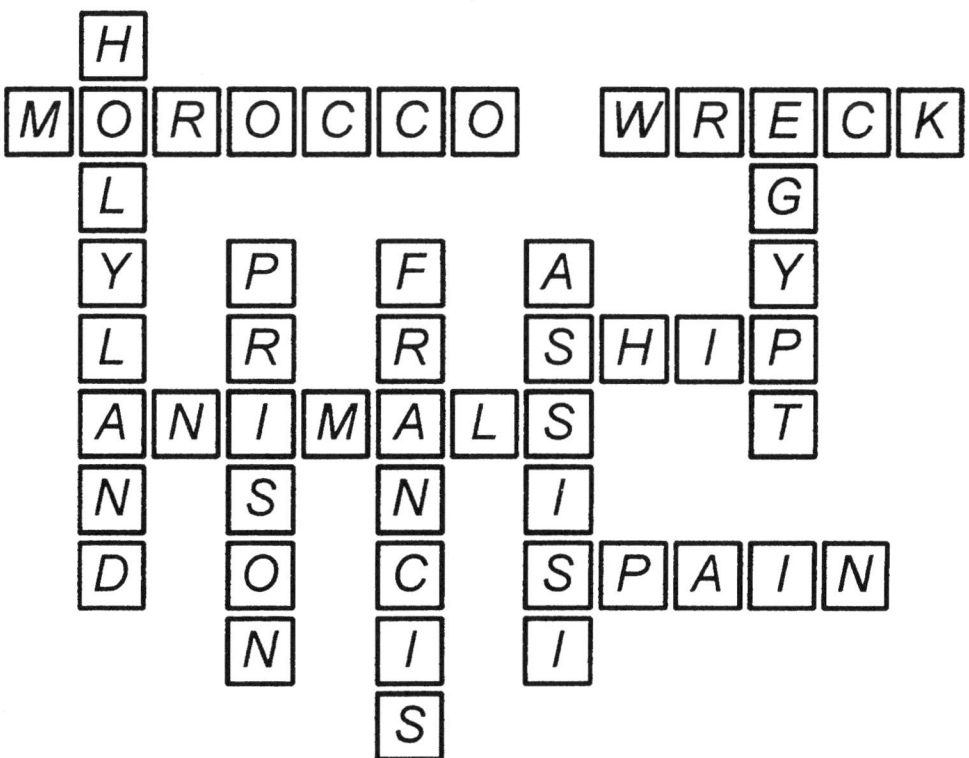

LIFE'S JOURNEY

Lesson 18

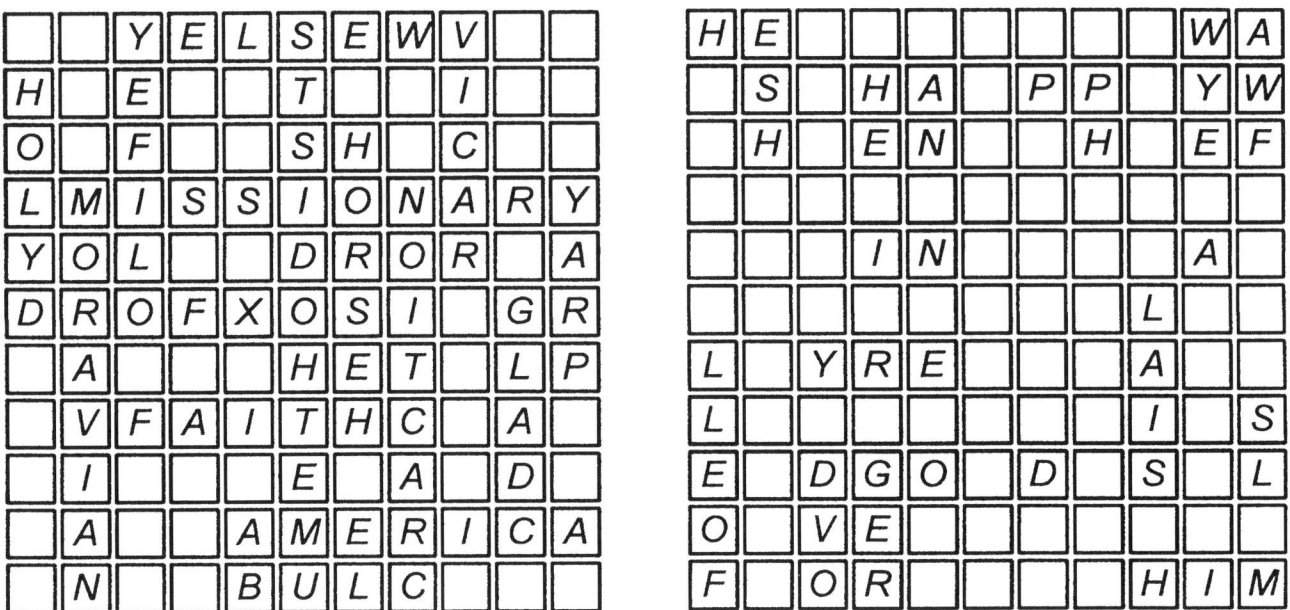

He was happy when he finally realised God's love for him.

Lesson 19

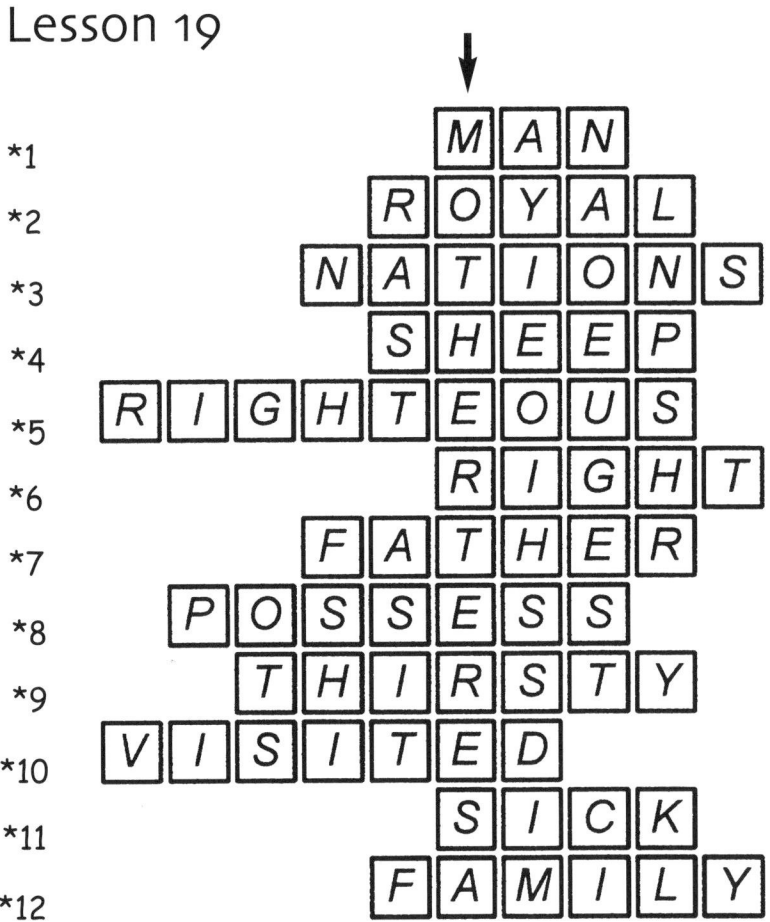

The words are: Mother Teresa

ANSWERS

Lesson 20

Put a number by each statement to show which Commandment it refers to.

10 Don't be greedy.

9 Be honest in all you say about people.

2 If we worship any idol (or anybody or anything else) we cannot be really dedicated to God.

3 God is great, and cares for us. We should never use his name wrongly.

1 God made us, and wants us to appreciate him, and give him the honour that he deserves.

5 People who despise the guidance of parents usually become bad adults.

6 We must realise and appreciate the value of every other person, even the ones we don't like.

4 God who made us knows how we work best. We need time for prayer and rest.

7 Realise the value of marriage and family life. No one should ever do anything that can damage it.

8 It belongs to someone else, so I will not take it from her or him.

The letters spell out: Keep the commandments for peace with all.

LIFE'S JOURNEY

Lesson 21

About God 1-4; about people 5-10.

'Love the Lord your God with all your heart, soul, mind and strength, and love your neighbour as yourself.'

Lesson 22

A = 2,3
B = 7
C = 4
D = 9
E = 5
F = 8
G = 1
H = 2,3
I = 6

Lesson 23

The fruit of the Spirit is . . .
love, joy, peace,
patience, kindness,
goodness, faithfulness,
humility and self-control.

Can the fruit of the Spirit be seen in your life?